Communications in Computer and Information Science 2107

Rationale

The CCIS series is devoted to the publication of proceedings of computer science conferences. Its aim is to efficiently disseminate original research results in informatics in printed and electronic form. While the focus is on publication of peer-reviewed full papers presenting mature work, inclusion of reviewed short papers reporting on work in progress is welcome, too. Besides globally relevant meetings with internationally representative program committees guaranteeing a strict peer-reviewing and paper selection process, conferences run by societies or of high regional or national relevance are also considered for publication.

Topics

The topical scope of CCIS spans the entire spectrum of informatics ranging from foundational topics in the theory of computing to information and communications science and technology and a broad variety of interdisciplinary application fields.

Information for Volume Editors and Authors

Publication in CCIS is free of charge. No royalties are paid, however, we offer registered conference participants temporary free access to the online version of the conference proceedings on SpringerLink (http://link.springer.com) by means of an http referrer from the conference website and/or a number of complimentary printed copies, as specified in the official acceptance email of the event.

CCIS proceedings can be published in time for distribution at conferences or as post-proceedings, and delivered in the form of printed books and/or electronically as USBs and/or e-content licenses for accessing proceedings at SpringerLink. Furthermore, CCIS proceedings are included in the CCIS electronic book series hosted in the SpringerLink digital library at http://link.springer.com/bookseries/7899. Conferences publishing in CCIS are allowed to use Online Conference Service (OCS) for managing the whole proceedings lifecycle (from submission and reviewing to preparing for publication) free of charge.

Publication process

The language of publication is exclusively English. Authors publishing in CCIS have to sign the Springer CCIS copyright transfer form, however, they are free to use their material published in CCIS for substantially changed, more elaborate subsequent publications elsewhere. For the preparation of the camera-ready papers/files, authors have to strictly adhere to the Springer CCIS Authors' Instructions and are strongly encouraged to use the CCIS LaTeX style files or templates.

Abstracting/Indexing

CCIS is abstracted/indexed in DBLP, Google Scholar, EI-Compendex, Mathematical Reviews, SCImago, Scopus. CCIS volumes are also submitted for the inclusion in ISI Proceedings.

How to start

To start the evaluation of your proposal for inclusion in the CCIS series, please send an e-mail to ccis@springer.com.

Cédric Grueau · Armanda Rodrigues ·
Lemonia Ragia

Editors

Geographical Information Systems Theory, Applications and Management

9th International Conference, GISTAM 2023
Prague, Czech Republic, April 25–27, 2023
Revised Selected Papers

 Springer

Editors
Cédric Grueau
Polytechnic Institute of Setúbal/IPS
Setúbal, Portugal

Armanda Rodrigues ⓘD
NOVA School of Science and Technology
Caparica, Portugal

Lemonia Ragia
Hellenic Open University
Patra, Greece

ISSN 1865-0929   ISSN 1865-0937 (electronic)
Communications in Computer and Information Science
ISBN 978-3-031-60276-4   ISBN 978-3-031-60277-1 (eBook)
https://doi.org/10.1007/978-3-031-60277-1

This Springer imprint is published by the registered company Springer Nature Switzerland AG
The registered company address is: Gewerbestrasse 11, 6330 Cham, Switzerland

Paper in this product is recyclable.

Preface

The present book includes extended and revised versions of a set of selected papers from the 9th International Conference on Geographical Information Systems Theory, Applications and Management (GISTAM 2023), held in Prague, Czech Republic, from 25–27 April.

GISTAM 2023 received 39 paper submissions from 23 countries, of which 15% were included in this book.

Papers were initially submitted to a double-blind review by at least three reviewers and their extended versions were submitted to a blind review by two reviewers. The conference accepted 25 papers of which six were selected to be extended and published in the current book. The papers were selected by the event chairs based on a number of criteria that included the classifications and comments provided by the program committee members, the session chairs' assessment and also the program chairs' global view of all papers included in the technical program. The authors of selected papers were then invited to submit revised and extended versions of their papers having at least 30% innovative material.

The International Conference on Geographical Information Systems Theory, Applications and Management aims to create a meeting point of researchers and practitioners that address new challenges in geo-spatial data sensing, observation, representation, processing, visualization, sharing and managing, in all aspects concerning both information communication and technologies (ICT) as well as management information systems and knowledge-based systems. The conference welcomes original papers of either practical or theoretical nature, presenting research or applications, of specialized or interdisciplinary nature, addressing any aspect of geographic information systems and technologies.

The papers selected to be included in this book contribute to the understanding of relevant trends of current research on Geographical Information Systems Theory, Applications and Management, including: Decision Support Systems, RADAR and LiDAR, Spatial Modeling and Reasoning, Urban and Regional Planning, Geospatial Information and Technologies, Geospatial Architectures and Middleware, Geocomputation, Energy Information Systems, Ecological and Environmental Management and Disaster Management.

We would like to thank all the authors for their contributions and also the reviewers who have helped to ensure the quality of this publication.

April 2023

Cédric Grueau
Armanda Rodrigues
Lemonia Ragia

Organization

Conference Chair

Lemonia Ragia   Hellenic Open University, Greece

Program Co-chairs

Cédric Grueau   Setubal Polytechnic University, Portugal
Armanda Rodrigues   NOVA University Lisbon, Portugal

Program Committee

Thierry Badard	Laval University, Canada
Pete Bettinger	University of Georgia, USA
Jan Blachowski	Wroclaw University of Science and Technology, Poland
Valeria C. T. Alves	Federal University of Pernambuco, Brazil
Pedro Cabral	Nanjing University of Information Science and Technology, China
Cristina Catita	Faculdade de Ciências da Universidade de Lisboa, Portugal
Filiberto Chiabrando	Politecnico di Torino, Italy
Eliseo Clementini	University of L'Aquila, Italy
Antonio Corral	University of Almería, Spain
Cyril de Runz	University of Tours, France
Vincenzo Di Pietra	Politecnico di Torino, Italy
Anastasios Doulamis	National Technical University of Athens, Greece
Max Egenhofer	University of Maine, USA
João Fernandes	Universidade de Lisboa, Portugal
Cheng Fu	University of Zurich, Switzerland
Sébastien Gadal	Aix-Marseille University, CNRS ESPACE UMR 7300, France and North Eastern Federal University, Russia
Ioannis Gitas	Aristotle University of Thessaloniki, Greece
Gil Gonçalves	University of Coimbra & INESC Coimbra, Portugal

Amy Griffin	RMIT University, Australia
Hans Guesgen	Massey University, New Zealand
Stephen Hirtle	University of Pittsburgh, USA
Wen-Chen Hu	University of North Dakota, USA
Simon Jirka	52°North, Germany
Roberto Lattuada	myHealthbox, Italy
Vladimir Lukin	Kharkov Aviation Institute, Ukraine
Jean Mas	Universidad Nacional Autónoma de México, Mexico
Gavin McArdle	University College Dublin, Ireland
Gintautas Mozgeris	Vytautas Magnus University, Lithuania
Anand Nayyar	Duy Tan University, Vietnam
Dimos Pantazis	University of West Attica, Greece
Cesar Parcero-Oubiña	Spanish National Research Council (CSIC), Spain
Mathieu Roche	Cirad, France
John Samuel	Graduate School of Chemistry, Physics and Electronics, Lyon, France
Diego Seco	Universidade da Coruña, Spain
Sylvie Servigne	INSA Lyon, France
Yosio Shimabukuro	Instituto Nacional de Pesquisas Espaciais, Brazil
Khairul Tahar	Universiti Teknologi MARA, Malaysia
Ana Teodoro	Oporto University, Portugal
Lorenzo Teppati Losè	Politecnico di Torino, Italy
Goce Trajcevski	Northwestern University, USA
Khalil Valizadeh Kamran	University of Tabriz, Iran
Benoit Vozel	University of Rennes I - IETR/Shine, France
Lei Wang	Louisiana State University, USA
Le Yu	Tsinghua University, China

Invited Speakers

Richard Lucas	Aberystwyth University, UK
Alexander Zipf	Heidelberg University, Germany
Costas Armenakis	York University, Canada

Contents

U-Nets and Multispectral Images for Detecting the Surface Water of Rivers via SAR Images

Diana Orlandi[1] , Federico A. Galatolo[1] , Alessandro La Rosa[2] ,
Mario G. C. A. Cimino[1](✉) , Pierfrancesco Foglia[1] , Carolina Pagli[2] ,
and Cosimo A. Prete[1]

[1] Department of Information Engineering, University of Pisa, Via G. Caruso 16, 56122 Pisa,
Italy
diana.orlandi@phd.unipi.it, {federico.galatolo,mario.cimino,
pierfrancesco.foglia,antonio.prete}@unipi.it
[2] Department of Earth Sciences, University of Pisa, Via Santa Maria 53, 56126 Pisa, Italy
alessandro.larosa@dst.unipi.it, carolina.pagli@unipi.it

Abstract. Global water resources are under increasing pressure due to demands
from population growth and climate change. As a result, the regime of the rivers
is changing and their ecosystems are threatened. Therefore, for effective water
management and mitigation of hazards, it is crucial to frequently and accurately
map the surface area of river water. Synthetic Aperture Radar (SAR) backscatter
images at high temporal resolution are nowadays available. However, mapping
the surface water of narrow water bodies, such as rivers, remains challenging due
to the SAR spatial resolution (few tens of meters). Conversely, Multi-Spectral
Instrument (MSI) images have a higher spatial resolution (few meters) but are
affected by cloud coverage. In this paper, we present a new method for automatic
detection and mapping of the surface water of rivers. The method is based on the
convolutional neural network known as U-Net. To develop the proposed approach,
two datasets are needed: (i) a set of Sentinel-2 MSI images, used to achieve target
values; (ii) a set of Sentinel-1A SAR backscatter images, used as input values. The
proposed method has been experimented to map the surface water of the Mijares
river (Spain) from April 2019 to September 2022. Experimental results show that
the proposed approach computes the total surface area covered by the river water
with a mean absolute error equal to 0.072, which is very promising for the target
application. To encourage scientific collaborations, the source code used for this
work has been made publicly available.

Keywords: Surface water of rivers · Synthetic aperture radar · Multispectral
images · Convolutional neural network · U-Net

1 Introduction

In the current era of global warming and climate change, a detailed and constant monitoring of the surface water of rivers is key not only for the correct estimation and
management of river regimes but also for the mitigation of flooding risks. In the literature, free and open access Synthetic Aperture Radar (SAR) backscatter images, acquired

C. Grueau et al. (Eds.): GISTAM 2023, CCIS 2107, pp. 1–13, 2024.
https://doi.org/10.1007/978-3-031-60277-1_1

at frequent revisit times, have been successfully applied to monitor changes of spatially large and broad surface water bodies, such as wetland and flooded areas [1–5]. However, mapping the surface extent of river water and its changes in time remains challenging [6] as some rivers are relatively narrow compared to the spatial resolution of SAR images (few tens of meters). In contrast, Multi-Spectral Instrument (MSI) data can offer spatial resolution on the order of a few meters, allowing for a more detailed mapping of the surface area of river water globally. However, MSI data are often affected by atmospheric noise and cloud coverage, which prevents regular observations. On the other hand, SAR satellites are capable of penetrating the atmosphere and measuring the radar backscattered from the surface of the Earth during day, night and all-weather conditions [7].

Modern deep learning techniques provide nowadays impressive results for detailed mapping and identification of features in images [8]. Recently, deep learning has shown great potential when applied to SAR data for the classification of sea and ice water, as well as for the surface water of rivers [9, 10]. In particular, the U-Net convolutional network is capable of resolving the extent of surface water bodies [11, 12], by combining a semantic segmentation upon partitioning of the input image into several regions corresponding to different classes (surface water, vegetation, buildings, and so on). More recently, a U-Net was experimented to detect the surface water of a narrow river [13]. For image segmentation, depending on the type of target to recognize, the U-Net architecture provides a spatial attention mechanism that allows highlighting only the relevant parts of the image during the initial training phase, thus limiting the computational resources, resulting in a better generalization capability [13].

In this research work, an experimental study is presented and discussed, in which a U-Net architecture has been trained to return the surface water of the Mijares river in Eastern Spain. The target dataset is made via MSI images, to generate the target surface water of the river, whereas the input dataset is made via SAR backscatter images. Additional images of both datasets have been used for testing. Overall, the experiment shows that a U-Net architecture achieves adequate accuracy for the target application.

2 Study Area

Mijares is a river that flows for about 156 km in a SE direction, south of the city of Castellón de la Plana, in Eastern Spain (Fig. 1). The river is fed by two major water springs, Mas Royo and Babor in the Sierra de Gudar. Despite the permanent nature of the river, its annual regime is irregular with lows in water flow in summers and floods in autumn [14]. For this study, we focused on the last 20 km of the river (Fig. 1) where Mijares flows across its alluvial plain [15]. This area is characterized by meandering sequences of fine to coarse sediments, which grade to deltaic sequences in the Almazora and Buriana plains. The alluvial deposits host the three main groundwater reservoirs of Arenoso (93 Mm^3), Sichar (49 Mm^3) and Maria Cristina (18.4 hm^3) [15, 16].

Since the 1960s, this part of the river and its associated reservoirs have been exploited for the agricultural, industrial, and urban activities of the region, as well as for the main water supply of the Sichar dam (0.2 Mm^3) [14]. However, as a result of the changing climate [15, 17], the region is recently experiencing warmer seasons, with the total rainfall between 1980 and 2012 having decreased by 3–7% compared to the previous period, 1940–2012 [16]. Currently, the water resources in the areas are 335.7 hm^3/year and must face a water demand of 268.23 hm^3/year [18]. Furthermore, during the latest years a series of historical records in flooding events have been reached, with such events being forecasted to occur more frequently in the future [19].

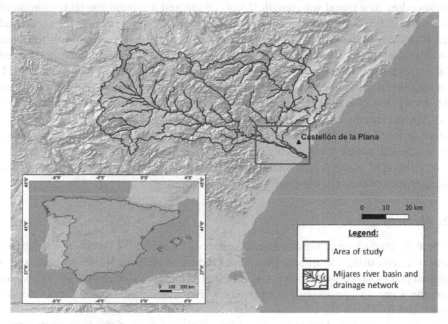

Fig. 1. Study area (red rectangle) and river drainage network [13] (Color figure online)

3 Material and Methods

3.1 Dataset

Two independent datasets are used, consisting of MSI and SAR backscatter images acquired by the ESA satellites Sentinel-2 and Sentinel-1A, respectively. The MSI images, acquired at 10 m spatial resolution, are used to derive maps of the surface water of the Mijares river during 2019–2022. Such maps are used as target output values for the convolutional neural network. The SAR backscattered images are used as corresponding input values.

The MSI dataset of the Mijares river consists of 36 Level 1C Sentinel-2 Multispectral images spanning the time-period between October 2019 and August 2022. In particular, the Level 1C images contain the spectral reflectance of 13 bands (B1–B12) acquired in the visible, near infrared (NIR) and short-wave infrared (SWIR) bands. The spatial resolution of the Sentinel-2 images varies between 10 m to 60 m, depending on the spectral band. In this study, bands B3 (green) and B8 (NIR) are used at a spatial resolution of 10 m. The 36 images selected have the lowest cloud coverage.

The SAR dataset consists of 36 Single Look Complex (SLC) images of the Mijares river, covering the time period between October 2019 and August 2022, and acquired from the descending orbit 008, in Interferometric Wide (IW) swath beam mode.

The Sentinel-1A SAR satellite has a revisit time of 12 days and it operates in C-band, corresponding to a signal wavelength (λ) of 5.6 cm and a ground spatial resolution of 5 m $\times$ 20 m [20]. The SAR signal contains two fundamental components of the polarized radar backscattered from the Earth surface: the amplitude and the phase. While the latter provides information about the targets positions on the ground, the amplitude can be used to investigate other targets properties, such as geometry, roughness, and wetness [21]. This makes the amplitude suitable for the detection of water bodies and flooded areas [11]. As a consequence, in this study, SAR amplitude images are used. In addition, in order to minimize the effect of thermal noise and maximize the signal backscatter from narrow surfaces of river water, the VV (Vertical Emitted-Vertical Received) polarization is selected, which is commonly characterized by stronger backscatter values than the VH (Vertical Emitted-Horizontal Received) polarization [22]. A summary of the characteristics of the two datasets is reported in Table 1.

3.2 Methods

In the following chapter, we describe the proposed method for detecting the surface water of ricers, using the BPMN (Business Process Model and Notation) language, a standard graphical representation for workflows [23]. Figure 1 shows the workflows for using the water surface detector in a periodical river assessment (a) and for developing the detector itself (b).

Specifically, in Fig. 1a the *detection of the water surface of the river* starts on the left, every detection period, by collecting periodical data on the river. After a number of historical data, during the assessment period a *report is generated*. The report is *checked and annotated by an expert*, and *sent to a Decision Support System* (DSS).

The core technology of the workflow in Fig. 2a is the water surface detector, which is developed for a given river according to the workflow of Fig. 2b. Specifically, the development workflow starts when there is a *new river to monitor* (on top left in figure). As a consequence, two parallel activities are carried out, i.e., *get MSI image and get SAR image*, respectively. Each type of image is followed by a different sequence of tasks. The next two subsections illustrate the two kinds of data ingestion and preparation.

MSI Image Ingestion and Preparation
A number of MSI images are first collected from the Sentinel-2 web service. Subsequently, to *enhance the water feature*, the Normalized Difference Water Index (NDWI) is calculated, using the spectral reflectance of B3 and B8 bands, as follows [24]:

$$NDWI = \frac{(B3 - B8)}{(B3 + B8)} \qquad (1)$$

In the formula, the combination of visible green (B3) and near-infrared (B8) bands highlights the water content of different water bodies [24]. In the resulting NDWI maps,

Table 1. Sentinel datasets.

Satellite	Sentinel-2	Sentinel-1A
Product Level	Multispectral Instrument (MSI) – Level-1C	Single Look Complex (SLC)
Tiles	T31TBE, T30TYK	–
Spatial Resolution (m)	10 × 10	5 × 20
Orbit	–	Descending (path 8, frame 458)
Acquisition mode	–	Interferometric Wide swath (IW)
Revisit time	–	12 days
Polarization	–	VV

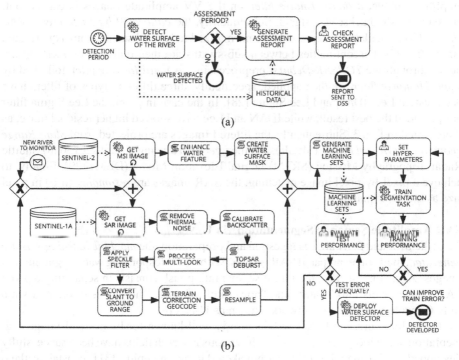

Fig. 2. The BPMN workflows for detecting the surface water of rivers: (a) the workflow for developing the detector; (b) the workflow for using the detector in a periodical river assessment.

a pixel value can vary between −1 and +1, with lower values corresponding to non-aqueous surfaces (soil or vegetation) and higher values corresponding to water. Finally, to *create the water surface mask* of the river, the pixels with NDWI values larger than a threshold are selected. In the case of the Mijares river, 36 MSI images are selected, and the threshold is set to −0.1. This threshold is found by comparing each of the 36 NDWI maps to its corresponding optical image, where the surface water of the Mijares river can be seen directly. As a result, 36 masks with two classes of surfaces, "water" and "non-water" are provided, 28 for training and 8 for testing.

In addition, to reduce the computational cost of the U-Net training, a single Water Surface Mask (WSM) of the river is created for the entire study period, by selecting pixels classified as "water" in at least one NDWI image. The WSM is helpful to keep only the water pixels related to the river, instead of considering the whole study area.

SAR Backscatter Image Ingestion and Preparation

The SAR SLCs backscatter images are first collected from the Sentinel-1A web service. Subsequently, a series of pre-processing steps are carried out via the Sentinel Application Platform [25]. Specifically, a number of corresponding SAR amplitude images are acquired in the same time window selected for the MSI images. Then, for each SAR amplitude image, *a thermal noise filter* on the VV amplitude images is carried out, normalizing the backscatter signal. Subsequently, the *calibrated backscattered coefficient* ($\sigma 0$) is calculated: it represents the normalized radar backscatter from a distributed target [26, 27]. Discontinuities between sub-swaths are then removed by merging the bursts through the *TOPSAR-Deburst* preprocessing. A *multi-looking filter* followed by a *speckle noise filter* are then applied: specifically, three different types of filters have been tested: Lee, IDAN and Lee Sigma [28]. In the case in point, the Lee Sigma filter has provided the best result, while IDAN and Lee have showed higher residual noise, as represented in Fig. 3. Subsequently, the filtered images are projected from *Slant Range geometry to Ground Range* (SRGR), and then *geocoded* using a 1 arc-sec (30 m) Shuttle Radar Topography Mission (SRTM) Digital Elevation Model (DEM) [29]. Finally, to achieve a pixel-by-pixel image matching, the SAR images are *resampled* to 10 m pixel size as the MSI images.

SAR Amplitude Semantic Segmentation via U-Net

After the MSI and SAR images ingestion and preparation, the *machine learning sets are generated*, made of 36 prepared SAR images, with 36 corresponding water segmentation images. As a consequence, the image segmentation task consists in separating a given SAR image pixels into "water" and "non-water" classes. The task is developed via a fully Convolutional Neural Network, known as U-Net [8].

In the literature, the U-Net architecture is well-known for biomedical image segmentation, but widespread applications in various research fields have been successfully developed: forest mapping [30], earthquakes damage mapping [31], coastal wetland classification [32], and so on. A U-Net exhibits a low computational demand, an accurate segmentation compared to other approaches, and a superior capability of working with a small training dataset [8].

An important step related to the U-Net development is the *setting of hyperparameters*. A detailed description of the final U-Net hyperparameters settings achieved for the Mijares river is presented in Table 2. It is worth noting that the hyperparameters setting is an iterative task, carried out after an improvement/optimization process, strongly depending on the complexity of the machine learning set.

In the subsequent *training of the segmentation task*, the U-Net optimizes its internal parameters to improve the mapping between the input samples (i.e., the 28 prepared SAR

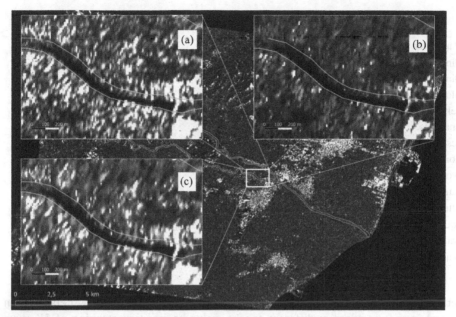

Fig. 3. SAR backscatter image of the Mijares river (background image) and detail of the SAR backscatter image after speckle filtering: (a) SAR backscatter image after Lee filter; (b) SAR backscatter image after IDAN filter; (c) SAR backscatter image after Lee Sigma [13].

backscatter images) and the corresponding target output samples (i.e., the 28 water/non-water surface maps generated from MSI images).

Specifically, the U-Net calculates the probability that a pixel belongs to a class. For this purpose, the U-Net adopts an encoding path that detects the features from the input dataset, and a decoding path that generates the output segmentation map. Both the encoding and decoding paths consist of a series of layers that are repeatedly applied on randomly sampled kernels of both the input dataset and the training dataset. In particular, the encoding path consists of a convolutional layer and a max pooling layer, which reduces the spatial dimension of the input maps multiple times, allowing the network to capture increasingly complex features. For the convolution operation, 128 × 128 pixels kernels are used. The decoding path initially applies an up-convolutional layer, which increases the spatial dimensions of the feature maps. Subsequently, it concatenates the output with the corresponding feature map obtained from the encoding path. This allows the network to compare the low-level and high-level features. This process of up-convolution and concatenation is repeated multiple times, allowing the network to refine the segmentation map.

The final output is a segmented image that assigns a class to each pixel in the input image. In the case in point, the segmented image is a map of the surface water of the Mijares river, where pixels pertaining to surface water of the river have a value of 1, while the other pixels are 0.

For the segmentation task of the Mijares river, the training phase is made by a subset of 28 of the 36 total images, while the remaining 8 images are used for testing. The

Table 2. U-Net hyperparameters settings [13].

Parameter	Description	Value(s)
dim	no. initial channels	8
dim mults	no. channels multipliers	[1, 2, 4]
blocks per stage	no. convolutional operations per stage	[2, 2, 2]
self-attentions per stage	no. self-attention blocks per stage	[0, 0, 1]
channels	input channels	1
resnet groups	no. normalization groups	2
consolidate upsample fmaps	feature maps consolidation	true
weight standardize	weight standardization	false
attention heads	no. attention heads	2
attention dim head	size of attention head	16
training window size	window size of training samples	128
training batch size	no. of samples per iteration	32
learning rate	amount of weight change in response to the error	0.001

performance of the predictions has been sampled between 5K and 50K iterations, on 10 test images acquired at different epochs, using an iteration stepping of 5K runs. Figure 4 illustrates some significant examples of mapping of the surface water of the Mijares river. In particular, Fig. 4a and Fig. 4b show the SAR image on Jan 20, 2020 and the corresponding MSI optical image (i.e., with lowest cloud coverage), on Feb 10, 2020, respectively. It is worth remembering that optical images are often affected by atmospheric noise and cloud coverage, which prevents regular observations. Figure 4c and Fig. 4d show the MSI-derived target output of the surface water (black), on Feb 10, 2020, and the Water Surface Mask generated for the entire study period via the training set, respectively. Finally, Fig. 3e and Fig. 3f illustrate the outputs of the U-Net on Jan 20, 2020, after 5K and 20K iterations, respectively: as the number of the iterations increases, the map of the surface water includes more details.

After *training the segmentation task*, in Fig. 2b the workflow continues with the performance evaluation: if the error can be improved, the hyperparameters setting is repeated, and so on. Otherwise, the U-Nete is evaluated on the test set: if the test error is adequate, the water surface detector is finally deployed and ready for use in the periodical river assessment. Otherwise, the workflow restarts from the beginning, by collecting a new data set.

4 Performance Evaluation and Discussion

To carry out the experimentation of the proposed research, an open-source implementation of the U-Net has been exploited [33] to develop the workflow of Fig. 2b. To encourage scientific collaborations, the source code used for this work has been made publicly available [34].

In Fig. 5 the graph of the cross-entropy loss vs. number of iterations is represented, for the first 30K iterations. The figure highlights that the training performance is effective after 5K iterations.

In order to measure the effectiveness of the approach, the total surface area covered by river water has been calculated, hereafter referred to as Normalized River Water Extent (NRWE), for both SAR and MSI timeseries. Figure 6 shows an excerpt of the two timeseries, with a clear similar progress. Overall, the Mean Absolute Error (MAE) between the SAR and MSI based NRWE is equal to 0.072, which is very effective for the target application.

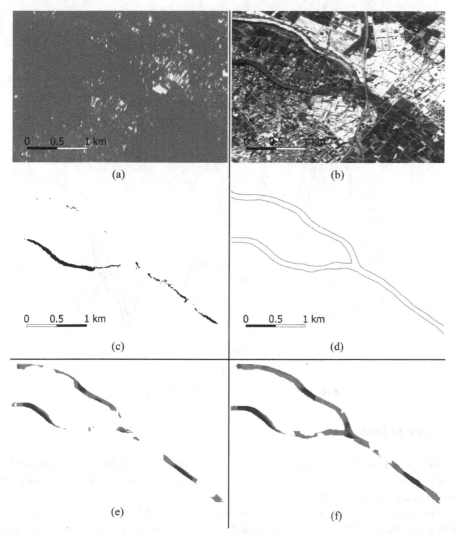

(a)　　　　　　　　　　　　　　　(b)

(c)　　　　　　　　　　　　　　　(d)

(e)　　　　　　　　　　　　　　　(f)

Fig. 4. Example of mapping of the surface water of the Mijares river: (a) Sentinel-1 SAR backscatter input image acquired on Jan 20, 2020; (b) Sentinel-2 MSI optical image acquired on Feb 10, 2020; (c) target output of the surface water (black) derived from NDWI map, calculated via the MSI image acquired on Feb 10, 2020; (d) Water Surface Mask generated via the training set; (e) output of the U-Net on Jan 20,2020 after 5K iterations; (f) output of the U-Net on Jan 20, 2020 after 20K iterations.

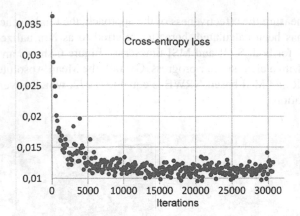

Fig. 5. Cross-entropy loss vs number of iterations [13].

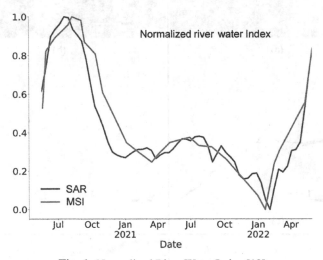

Fig. 6. Normalized River Water Index [13].

5   Conclusions

In this research work, the U-Net Convolutional Neural Network has been proposed to detect the surface water of rivers via satellite data, using MSI and SAR images as target and input data, respectively.

The paper illustrates the proposed method using the Mijares river in Spain as a pilot study area. For the sake of reproducibility, a workflow has been formalized and illustrated in BPMN language, to detail the Sentinel datasets and their preprocessing, the development of the U-Net for the segmentation task, the hyperparameters settings, as well as the periodical river monitoring for feeding a decision support system.

The experimental studies on the Mijares river are promising, with a mean absolute error of the total water surface area equal to 0.072, although the presented approach represents an initial step towards a more comprehensive experimentation.

Further investigations can involve the extension of the time period of analysis, with the aim of monitoring the temporal fluctuations and climate change impacts on river ecosystems. To encourage scientific collaborations, the source code used for this work has been made publicly available [34].

Acknowledgements. This work has been partially supported by: (i) the National Center for Sustainable Mobility MOST/Spoke10, funded by the Italian Ministry of University and Research, in the framework of the National Recovery and Resilience Plan; (ii) the PRA_2022_101 project "Decision Support Systems for territorial networks for managing ecosystem services", funded by the University of Pisa; (iii) the Ministry of University and Research (MUR) as part of the PON 2014–2020 "Research and Innovation" resources – "Green/Innovation Action – DM MUR 1061/2022"; (iv) the Italian Ministry of University and Research (MUR), in the framework of the "Reasoning" project, PRIN 2020 LS Programme, Project number 2493 04–11–2021; (v) the Italian Ministry of Education and Research (MIUR) in the framework of the FoReLab project (Departments of Excellence).

References

1. Botha, E.J., Anstee, J.M., Sagar, S., Lehmann, E., Medeiros, T.A.G.: Classification of Australian waterbodies across a wide range of optical water types. Remote Sens. **12** (2020). https://doi.org/10.3390/RS12183018
2. Frappart, F., et al.: Automatic detection of inland water bodies along altimetry tracks for estimating surface water storage variations in the congo basin. Remote Sens. **13**, 1–22 (2021). https://doi.org/10.3390/rs13193804
3. Carreño-Conde, F., De Mata Muñoz, M.: Flood monitoring based on the study of Sentinel-1 SAR images: the Ebro River case study. Water (Switzerland). **11**, 1–25 (2019). https://doi.org/10.3390/w11122454
4. Quirós, E., Gagnon, A.S.: Validation of flood risk maps using open source optical and radar satellite imagery. Trans. GIS **24**, 1208–1226 (2020). https://doi.org/10.1111/tgis.12637
5. Tran, K.H., Menenti, M., Jia, L.: Surface water mapping and flood monitoring in the Mekong delta using sentinel-1 SAR time series and Otsu threshold. Remote Sens. **14** (2022). https://doi.org/10.3390/rs14225721
6. Filippucci, P., Brocca, L., Bonafoni, S., Saltalippi, C., Wagner, W., Tarpanelli, A.: Sentinel-2 high-resolution data for river discharge monitoring. Remote Sens. Environ. **281**, 113255 (2022). https://doi.org/10.1016/j.rse.2022.113255
7. Kumar, D.: Urban objects detection from C-band synthetic aperture radar (SAR) satellite images through simulating filter properties. Sci. Rep. **11**, 6241 (2021). https://doi.org/10.1038/s41598-021-85121-9
8. Ronneberger, O., Fisher, P., Brox, T.: Convolutional networks for biomedical image segmentation. In: International Conference on Medical Image Computing and Computer-Assisted Intervention (2015). https://doi.org/10.48550/arXiv.1505.04597
9. Jiang, M., Xu, L., Clausi, D.A.: Sea ice–water classification of RADARSAT-2 imagery based on residual neural networks (ResNet) with regional pooling. Remote Sens. **14** (2022). https://doi.org/10.3390/rs14133025

10. Orlandi, D., Galatolo, F.A., Cimino, M.G.C.A., Rosa, A.La, Pagli, C., Perilli, N.: Enhancing land subsidence awareness via InSAR data and Deep Transformers. In: Proceedings - 2022 IEEE International Conference on Cognitive and Computational Aspects of Situation Management, CogSIMA 2022, pp. 98–103 (2022). https://doi.org/10.1109/CogSIMA54611.2022.9830661
11. Wang, G., Wu, M., Wei, X., Song, H.: Water identification from high-resolution remote sensing images based on multidimensional densely connected convolutional neural networks. Remote Sens. 12 (2020). https://doi.org/10.3390/rs12050795
12. Wang, J., et al.: FWENet: a deep convolutional neural network for flood water body extraction based on SAR images. Int. J. Digit. Earth. 15, 345–361 (2022). https://doi.org/10.1080/17538947.2021.1995513
13. Orlandi, D., et al.: Using deep learning and radar backscatter for mapping river water surface. In: Proceedings of the 9th International Conference on Geographical Information Systems Theory, Applications and Management - GISTAM, pp. 216–221. SciTePress (2023). https://doi.org/10.5220/0011975000003473. ISBN 978-989-758-649-1. ISSN 2184-500X
14. Macian-Sorribes H., Pulido-Velazquez M., Tilmant A.: Definition of efficient scarcity-based water pricing policies through stochastic programming. Hydrol. Earth Syst. Sci. 19, 3925–3935 (2015). https://doi.org/10.5194/hess-19-3925-2015. www.hydrol-earth-syst-sci.net/19/3925/2015
15. Garófano-Gómez, V., Martínez-Capel, F., Bertoldi, W., Gurnell, A., Estornell, J., Segura-Beltrán, F.: Six decades of changes in the riparian corridor of a mediterranean river: a synthetic analysis based on historical data sources. Ecohydrology 6, 536–553 (2013). https://doi.org/10.1002/eco.1330
16. MedECC: Spatial characterization of the seawater upcoming process in a coastal Mediterranean aquifer (Plana de Castellón, Spain): evolution and controls. In: Cramer, W., Guiot, J., Marini, K. (eds.) Union for the Mediterranean, Plan Bleu, UNEP/MAP, Marseille, France, p. 632 (2020). https://doi.org/10.1007/s12665-016-5531-7
17. MedECC: Climate and Environmental Change in the Mediterranean Basin – Current Situation and Risks for the Future. First Mediterranean Assessment Report (2020). https://doi.org/10.5281/zenodo.4768833
18. Confederación Hidrográfica del Júcar: Plan Hidrológico de la Demarcación Hidrográfica del Júcar. Revisión de tercer ciclo (2021–2027) (2019)
19. Masson-Delmotte, V., et al.: Summary for policymakers. In: Climate Change 2021: The Physical Science Basis. Contribution of Working Group I to the Sixth Assessment Report of the Intergovernmental Panel on Climate Change (2021)
20. Yague-Martinez, N., et al.: Interferometric processing of sentinel-1 TOPS data. IEEE Trans. Geosci. Remote Sens. 54, 2220–2234 (2016). https://doi.org/10.1109/TGRS.2015.2497902
21. Geudtner, D., Torres, R., Snoeij, P., Ostergaard, A., Navas-Traver, I.: Sentinel-1 mission capabilities and SAR system calibration. In: IEEE National Radar Conference - Proceedings 0–3 (2013). https://doi.org/10.1109/RADAR.2013.6586141
22. Dzurisin, D., Lu, Z.: Interferometric synthetic-aperture radar (InSAR). In: Volcano Deformation. Geodetic Monitoring Techniques, pp. 153–194. Springer, Heidelberg (2007). https://doi.org/10.1007/978-3-540-49302-0_5
23. Ciaramella, A., Cimino, M.G., Lazzerini, B., Marcelloni, F.: Using BPMN and tracing for rapid business process prototyping environments. In: International Conference on Enterprise Information Systems, vol. 1, pp. 206–212. SCITEPRESS (2009)
24. McFeeters, S.K.: The use of the Normalized Difference Water Index (NDWI) in the delineation of open water features. Int. J. Remote Sens. 25, 687–711 (1996). https://doi.org/10.1080/01431169608948714
25. SNAP - ESA Sentinel Application Platform v2.0.2. http://step.esa.int

26. Tamkuan, N., Nagai, M.: ALOS-2 and sentinel-1 backscattering coefficients for water and flood detection in Nakhon Phanom Province, northeastern Thailand. Int. J. Geoinformatics. **17**, 39–48 (2021). https://doi.org/10.52939/ijg.v17i3.1895
27. Laur, H., et al.: Derivation of the backscattering coefficient in ESA ERS SAR PRI Products. In: ESA Document No: ES-TN-RS-PM-HL09 05, p. 53 (2004)
28. Tran, K.H., Menenti, M., Jia, L.: Surface water mapping and flood monitoring in the Mekong delta using sentinel-1 SAR time series and Otsu threshold. Remote Sens. **14**, 5721 (2022). https://doi.org/10.3390/rs14225721
29. Farr, T.G., et al.: The shuttle radar topography mission. Rev. Geophys. **45** (2007). https://doi.org/10.1029/2005RG000183
30. Wagner, F.H., et al.: Using the U-net convolutional network to map forest types and disturbance in the Atlantic rainforest with very high resolution images. Remote Sens. Ecol. Conserv. **5**, 360–375 (2019). https://doi.org/10.1002/rse2.111
31. Bai, Y., Mas, E., Koshimura, S.: Towards operational satellite-based damage-mapping using U-Net convolutional network: a case study of 2011 Tohoku Earthquake-Tsunami. Remote Sens. **10** (2018). https://doi.org/10.3390/rs10101626
32. Dang, K.B., et al.: Coastal wetland classification with deep U-Net convolutional networks and sentinel-2 imagery: a case study at the Tien Yen Estuary of Vietnam. Remote Sens. **12**, 1–26 (2020). https://doi.org/10.3390/rs12193270
33. Wang, P.: Implementation of a Unet complete with efficient attention as well as the latest research findings (2023). https://github.com/lucidrains/x-unet
34. Galatolo, F.A.: Gistam2023 (2023). github.com/galatolofederico/gistam2023

A Combination of Geomatic Techniques for Modelling the Urban Environment in Virtual Reality

Claudio Spadavecchia(✉) ⓘ, Elena Belcore ⓘ, Vincenzo Di Pietra ⓘ,
and Nives Grasso ⓘ

DIATI, Politecnico di Torino, Corso Duca degli Abruzzi 24, 10129 Torino, Italy
{claudio.spadavecchia,elena.belcore,vincenzo.dipietra,
nives.grasso}@polito.it

Abstract. Historical city centres represent invaluable cultural and architectural heritage, often facing challenges such as neglect, urbanisation, and dwindling visitor engagement. Italian city centres are usually rich in historical buildings, statues and open-sky arts, causing difficulties in changing the urbanisation tissue and promoting infrastructural works in front of the citizens. Therefore, it is fundamental not only to document and survey the current state with geomatics techniques but also to propose engaging and educational experiences for citizens exploiting the potential of VR. In fact, VR offers an immersive and interactive medium that can bridge the gap between the past and the present, revitalising these urban gems while preserving their historical significance. This paper focuses on two aspects of historical city centres' digital documentation: (a) the geomatics integrated survey exploiting LiDAR and UAV photogrammetric techniques and (b) the process of optimising geomatics products into VR experiences. A big issue in transposing dense digital models into a VR environment is the information's weight, which prevents the app from running smoothly. We aim to comprehensively examine the potential, challenges, and best practices for processing surveying data at optimal efficiency with respect to a VR environment.

Keywords: VR environment · 3D model · Cultural heritage · LiDAR · UAS · Geomatic

1 Introduction

Historic city centres represent cultural and architectural treasures of immeasurable value [1]. They serve as custodians of history, reflecting traces of bygone eras through their architecture, streets, and monuments. These places captivate not only with their aesthetic beauty but also with their ability to tell stories, revealing the evolution of societies over time. The preservation of historic city centres is essential for safeguarding cultural diversity, promoting intercultural understanding, and providing a tangible connection to our past [2]. Furthermore, they contribute to sustainable tourism, fostering the conservation and appreciation of our heritage riches [3, 4]. Nowadays, Virtual Reality (VR) plays

C. Grueau et al. (Eds.): GISTAM 2023, CCIS 2107, pp. 14–33, 2024.
https://doi.org/10.1007/978-3-031-60277-1_2

a pivotal role in the preservation and promotion of cultural heritage [5–7]. It offers an immersive platform that allows individuals to step back in time and explore historical and cultural sites with unprecedented realism and interactivity. VR enables the creation of faithful digital replicas of heritage sites, artefacts, and artworks, ensuring their conservation for future generations [8–10]. Moreover, it enhances educational experiences by providing students and enthusiasts with dynamic, hands-on learning opportunities, making history and culture more engaging and accessible [11–13]. Additionally, VR contributes to the accessibility of cultural heritage, enabling individuals with physical limitations or geographical constraints to experience and appreciate these treasures [14]. By blending technology with culture, VR revolutionises how we engage with our past, fostering a deeper connection to our heritage and encouraging its preservation for posterity.

Virtual reality is a powerful technology that promises to change our lives [15] by simulating a virtual environment that immerses users to the extent that they have the feeling of "being there" [16]. In recent years, virtual reality has made a comeback mainly in the field of gaming and entertainment and is supported by low production costs and affordable retail prices; however, this technology is nowadays widely used in various research fields such as medicine [17–20], military purposes [21], and education [22]. More recently, this technology has been used for cultural heritage domain [23, 24] and tourist and informational purposes, such as virtual museum visits [25, 26], where users can virtually move between art installations and inspect them.

Recent studies have proposed procedures for taking advantage of three-dimensional photogrammetric or LiDAR models and recreating virtual reality environments [27, 28], mainly focusing on mesh generation and importing in a virtual environment. Nevertheless, to the best of our knowledge, no study describes the complete workflow to follow in a detailed and exhaustive way to acquire a georeferenced three-dimensional model to be imported and visualised in VR. Photogrammetry is the process of deriving metric information about an object through measurements made on object photographs [29]. This well-established methodology is widely used in civil engineering [30, 31], mapping [32] and 3D modelling [33, 34]. 3D modelling is a process that starts from data acquisition and ends with the final 3D virtual model [33], and it can now be considered one of the most important and attractive products of photogrammetry [35, 36]. Traditional 3D models are generated with aerial and/or terrestrial images [33, 37] according to consolidated Structure from Motion/Multi-View Stereo (SfM-MVS) workflows [38, 39]. However, with the advent of LiDAR (Light Detection and Ranging) as a commonly used instrument in the remote sensing field, new three-dimensional models are generated using this approach [40, 41] or by combining it with the photogrammetric procedure and according to standardised procedures [33, 42–44]. Nowadays, generating a 3D model through an integrated approach is preferred because of the ease of acquisition, mainly due to the photogrammetric part, and the simultaneous high accuracy due to the LiDAR survey.

When discussing VR experience with headset devices, it is important to build applications optimised enough to run smoothly on their target devices and avoid discomfort for the user [45]. This is particularly true when the developed application must reproduce digitally real objects to let the user interact with them [46]. Optimising a VR project is a complex task involving developers and artists to simulate the complex reality in a virtual environment. While modelling from scratch a digital asset unrelated to the physical world is a task related to digital artists, reconstructing existing objects, structures or environments is nowadays demanded to the potentiality of the photogrammetric process [47, 48]. With photogrammetry, creating extremely high-quality assets for non-VR usage is possible, mainly required in the engineering architecture and environment fields [49]. The workflow applied for photogrammetric reconstruction is primarily devoted to producing cartographic products like Digital Elevation Models (DTM) and Orthomosaic Maps. Point clouds are sometimes used to perform specific tasks like semantic segmentation, classification or 3D mapping [50]. In this panorama, the optimisation parameters are totally different concerning VR 3D modelling, as the photogrammetric model must ensure accurate geometric reconstruction for measuring and design and confident radiometric response for monitoring and documentation.

In this study, our goal is to fill the gap mentioned above, proposing a standardised workflow that describes the entire process necessary for the creation of a complete virtual environment, starting from the acquisition phase, passing through data processing and the generation of a three-dimensional model, and finalising it with export into virtual reality for educational purposes. In particular, we will go into depth about the photogrammetric products and highlight the difficulties encountered and the challenges to be overcome to optimise the result in the best possible way regarding quality and processing time. Specifically, we will propose a Virtual Reality outdoor environment recreating a city portion of Turin (Italy), including Carlo Alberto Square, Carignano Square, and Carignano Palace. Due to the historical value of this area, the final goal is to enhance and promote the cultural heritage from an artistic point of view, giving virtual reality a tourist, educational, and didactic purpose. This study is a natural continuation of our previous study [44], in which we had deepened the survey and post-processing phase but in which the implementation in a virtual environment had only been hinted at.

2 Materials and Methods

In this chapter, the study area is first introduced, and the methodology adopted is subsequently described in depth in terms of sensors and instrumentation used and how it was integrated to obtain a coherent final product, placing greater emphasis on photogrammetric processing and optimization for VR experience.

2.1 Survey Area

The survey area, as shown in Fig. 1, extends for about 21,000 m^2, and it includes Carignano Square, Carignano Palace, Carlo Alberto Square, Principe Amedeo Street and Cesare Battisti Street (both in the extension between Carignano Square and Carlo Alberto Square), Carlo Alberto Street (between Carlo Alberto Square and Po Street) and Po Street (between Castello Square and Giambattista Bogino Street). As highlighted in [44], the survey and the high-resolution 3D model generation were performed with the aim of implementing the model in a virtual environment and providing an interactive tool for the enhancement of the survey area and innovatively advertise citizens and tourist (with a greater level of detail on Palazzo Carignano and the statue of Carlo Alberto). Additional goals were (i) to provide support for the renovation of Carlo Alberto Square, where a station for the new underground city metro line will be realised; (ii) to measure the exact location of the statue dedicated to Carlo Alberto (placed in the homonymous square) which, to preserve its integrity, will be removed during the construction phase and subsequently placed back in the exact location; and (iii) to carry out further analyses concerning possible road interferences between the surface road network (in particular public transport by rail) and the planned underground road.

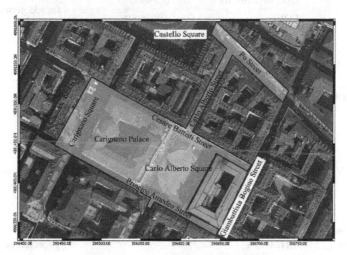

Fig. 1. Study area. EPSG: 32632 [44].

2.2 Materials

Table 1 summarises the sensors used during the survey. A DJI Mini Mavic drone was used to acquire rooftop images; the Riegl VZ-400i laser scanner combined with a Nikon D800E digital camera was used to acquire a dense coloured point cloud to reconstruct the façade geometries with high-resolution; finally, the texture generation in narrow streets was entrusted to a Ricoh Theta V 360° camera.

The topographic phase of the survey, fundamental to defining a standard reference coordinate system for harmonising data, was done with the support of two GNSS receivers (Leica GS14 and Leica GS18), which can receive both the GPS and GLONASS constellations. Also, a Leica Geosystem Image Station total station and prisms were needed to create a polygonal scheme consisting of 14 station points required to georeference the point cloud and the images acquired.

The VR experience populated with the digital model obtained by the integrated survey was developed using Unity software (Unity Technologies) and deployed in the Meta Quest Pro headset. Unity is a cross-platform game engine able to support Android platforms and customisation for headset VR applications. For this project, the Unity Editor version 2021.3.19f1 has been used.

Table 1. Specifications and purpose of the sensors used in the in-situ survey.

Sensor	Characteristics		Purpose
DJI Mini Mavic	Resolution	12 Mpx	Roofs modelling
	Focal Length	4 mm	
	Sensor	1/2.3″ CMOS	
RIEGL VZ-400i	Measure technique	ToF	High-detailed reconstruction of facade geometries
	Operative distance	0.5–800 m	
	FOV	100°/360°	
	Frequency	100/1200 Hz	
	Accuracy	5/3 mm	
	Size	206 × 308 mm	
NIKON D800E	Resolution	36.2 Mpx	High-detailed texture generation
	Focal Length	60 mm	
	Sensor	35,9 × 24,0 mm CMOS	
Ricoh Theta V	Resolution	12 Mpx (x2)	Texture generation for narrow streets
	Focal Length	1 mm	
	Sensor	1/2.3 CMOS (x2)	
Leica Geosystem Image Station	Angle measure accuracy 1 Hz and V	0.5″ (0.15 mgon)	Lidar and images georeferencing
Prisms	Reflective	Yes	
GS14 and GS18 GNSS receivers	GNSS Systems	Multi-frequency	

Meta Quest Pro is a mixed reality (MR) headset developed by Reality Labs, a division of Meta Platforms (formerly Facebook, Inc.). Meta Quest Pro has a resolution of 1832 * 1920 pixels per eye and a claimed field of view of 106° (horizontal) × 96° (vertical). Table 2 summarises the technological features of the headset.

2.3 Methods

Addressing the integration and optimisation process of 3D photogrammetric products for VR use requires dividing the workflow into two main steps: the execution of the integrated survey, exploiting the methods and techniques of geomatics, and the processing and manipulating of derived data for the VR experience.

Integrated Survey. The primary challenge in creating a high-detail, multi-scale, and versatile 3D model of a city lies in finding a compromise between the time spent on data acquisition and data processing. This involves a thorough analysis of the relationship between the area to be surveyed, the time required for surveying, and the careful selection

Table 2. Technical specs of Meta Quest Pro headset.

Sensor component	Characteristics
Operating system	Android
Headset processor	Qualcomm Snapdragon XR2+
Headset dimension	265 mm (length) × 127 mm (height) × 196 mm (width); 722 g (weight)
Display	LCD 1800 × 1920 per eye @ 72–90 Hz
Graphics	Adreno 650
Eye-tracking	5x IR imaging sensor (12° FOV)
Headset-tracking	10x imaging camera for 6 DoF SLAM inside-out
Storage memory	Western Digital 256 GB NAND flash
Memory (RAM)	Micron Technology 12 GB LPDDR5, SDRAM
Controller processor	2x Qualcomm Snapdragon 662, Arm-based, octo-core
Controller tracking	SLAM based on 5 imaging cameras

of appropriate sensors to ensure sufficient detail based on the survey objectives. Since the investigated area is characterised by various difficulties (i.e., walking area, flight restrictions, numerous architectural details), it was necessary to plan the survey carefully, in particular: (i) the UAS flight planning required careful consideration of factors such as proper overlap, correct resolution, adequate camera orientation, optimal acquisition time to minimise shadows on facades, and adhering to safety requirements in light of the high tourist activity in the area; (ii) the location, number, and resolution of TLS scans were carefully set to achieve a continuous surface with a consistent point density; (iii) the methodology for acquiring photos for texture reconstruction was constrained by the varying illumination conditions on the facades, adding to the complexity of the task. Consequently, multi-sensor and multi-scale approaches were necessary to fulfil these requirements. Some areas within the surveyed region may have greater significance, such as the Carignano Palace facade and Carlo Alberto's statue, compared to other buildings in Cesare Battisti and Principe Amedeo Streets. Combining optical and LiDAR sensors was considered to balance resolution demands and available resources. Figure 2 shows the workflow followed in this study.

In-situ Survey. The topographic network needed for georeferencing the acquired data was established comprising four vertices strategically positioned to ensure ample satellite visibility. The coordinates of these vertices were measured using GNSS instrumentation in rapid-static mode (Leica GS14 and Leica GS18), with each point stationed for one hour. The total station was also used to determine the position of specific reference points. This process led to the creating of a polygonal scheme comprising 14 station points. In addition, circular retroreflective artificial targets with a 5 cm radius were strategically placed along the facades and measured using the total station (Fig. 3). Due to the reflectivity information, these targets can be easily identified within the LiDAR point clouds. Furthermore, natural points with distinct features were also measured

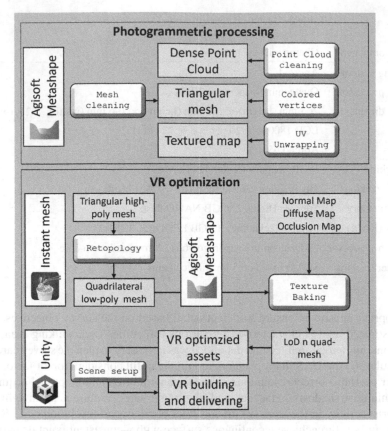

Fig. 2. Workflow of the paper.

(Fig. 3). Altogether, a total of 264 points were measured to enable the georeferencing of both LiDAR and photogrammetric acquisitions.

Fig. 3. Example of a retroreflective target (left) and natural point (right) [44].

42 LiDAR scans were needed to obtain a complete point cloud of the area. The acquisition frequency was set equal to 600 kHz (equivalent to an acquisition speed of approximately 250,000 points per second), and the angular resolution was carefully set to ensure a point was captured approximately every 6 mm at a distance of 10 m from

the station point. The combination with the NIKON digital camera allows the assigning of colour information to the point cloud.

The DJI Mini Mavic UAS was employed to conduct a high-resolution survey of the roofs with both nadiral and oblique views, ensuring complete coverage of the entire area and gathering detailed information about ceilings and walls for integration into the LiDAR model. The flight height was set at 40 m above the ground to achieve a Ground Sample Distance (GSD) of less than 2 cm. In total, 1,599 images were acquired during the survey.

Digital images from the ground at a high resolution, particularly for the facades of buildings, were needed to guarantee the high quality of the 3D model textures. To achieve this, approximately 400 images were captured using the NIKON D800E camera, employing a nadiral angle as close to the facades as possible. This data collection focused on the buildings facing the two squares and included Carlo Alberto's statue.

Data Processing. The GNSS data was post-processed in relative mode using the data from the GNSS Interregional Positioning Service (SPIN 3 GNSS) permanent network within the Leica Geo Office (LGO) software. For the reference cartographic grid, the UTM-WGS84 projection was chosen. However, a conventional local isometric system (MTL2 ISO250) was adopted to avoid typical cartographic representation distortions. Regarding the GNSS heights, they were measured above the ellipsoid and subsequently converted into orthometric heights using the "ITALGEO2005" geoid undulations model provided by the Italian Geographic Military Institute (Istituto Geografico Militare, IGM).

The compensation of the network using MicroSurvey Star*Net software resulted in an estimated coordinates standard deviation (RMSE) of less than 1 cm. To georeference the UAS photogrammetric products, specific Ground Control Points (GCPs) were marked and measured using GNSS receivers. The NRTK-GNSS method, with real-time centimetric precision, was utilised for these measurements, thanks to the corrections received from a local network of permanent SPIN 3 GNSS service stations. Photographic points easily identifiable in drone images, such as pavement edges, road markings, and corners of maintenance holes, were used for this purpose. The field-acquired coordinates were then exported using LGO software to obtain the final coordinates in the national geodetic reference system ETRF2000 with 32N UTM projection.

The data collected from the laser scanner and the topographic survey underwent post-processing using Riegl's RiScan Pro software. To achieve relative registration of scans and georeferencing in the absolute coordinate system, retroreflective targets were employed. Each target was associated with the actual coordinates measured during the topographic survey. The initial registration of scanning positions was performed semi-automatically based on voxel analysis. The identified targets in the scans served as additional observations for relative registration between scans, enhancing the accuracy of scan location estimation. Subsequently, further optimisation was carried out for relative registration between scans and georeferencing. This optimisation considered all the acquisitions made and available targets, GNSS measurements, and altitude measurements from the inertial platform. During this optimisation phase, flat patches representing the environment's surfaces were extracted from each scan. An iterative process was then used to seek homologous planes between different scans and establish their correspondence. This procedure permanently corrected the relative positions between the scans while simultaneously estimating the absolute position of the scans. As raw scan data typically lacks radiometric information, the Riegl VZ-400i relies on its digital camera, mounted on top of the instrument, to attribute colour information to each pixel. However, for this process, calibration data of the camera is required. Although the internal calibration of the camera is known in advance, recalibration of external parameters is necessary whenever the camera is mounted on the instrument. These external calibration parameters can be estimated by matching common points between the scan and the images acquired at the same station point. After this calibration process, each point in the cloud is coloured according to the corresponding pixels of the assigned calibrated images. Finally, the georeferenced point cloud, as shown in Fig. 4, was exported in.las format.

Fig. 4. Registered point cloud [44].

Regarding the photogrammetric procedure, all the images were processed using Agisoft Metashape Professional, a commercial software based on Structure-from-Motion (SfM) techniques. In the initial phase, a fully automatic alignment between images was performed to reconstruct the relative positions. A photogrammetric camera calibration was conducted to determine essential parameters such as the correct focal distance, main point position, sensor distortions, and radial and tangential optics. To generate a dense point cloud, the algorithm computes depth maps, which are derived through the application of dense stereo-matching techniques. These depth maps are computed by considering the relative exterior and interior orientation parameters of overlapping image pairs, estimated through bundle adjustment. Multiple depth maps are generated pairwise for each camera and subsequently merged to form a consolidated depth map. This merging process leverages the surplus information in the overlapping regions to eliminate inaccuracies in in-depth measurements. To improve accuracy, 10 Ground Control Points (GCPs) were manually selected and marked on various images. Among these, five were chosen as checkpoints (CPs) for validation purposes. The block compensation process resolved the residuals on GCPs and CPs, leading to the refinement of the camera calibration. As a result, the images were accurately positioned and oriented in space, ensuring alignment with the isometric coordinate system. To create the textured 3D model of the study area, the dense point clouds obtained from the procedures mentioned above were integrated, resulting in a comprehensive model of the urban environment. The dense cloud was then divided into seven distinct portions to be processed separately. A full resolution was chosen for the main buildings: Carignano

Palace, the National Library, and Carlo Alberto's statue. However, 1 to 5 cm resolution was used for buildings facing the square and terrain. The dense georeferenced models served as a basis for generating the 3D mesh, focusing on achieving a high-quality level maximising the number of triangles for optimal representation.

Photogrammetric Processing and Optimisation for VR Experience. This section is dedicated to applying photogrammetry in VR development, outlining the steps to bridge the divide between digital reconstruction and the optimisation necessary for virtual reality. The optimisation of a VR project is a multifaceted endeavour that requires collaboration between developers and artists to replicate intricate real-world scenarios within a virtual environment faithfully. The proposed workflow focuses on the photogrammetric processing and optimisation aspects of geometric and radiometric reconstruction. Other parameters unrelated to the photogrammetric procedure are not considered for this work. Shadowing, aliasing, mipmapping, and other optimisation aspect are strictly related to the digital artist choice and requires specific competence related to the game design and VR tools developers.

The proposed workflow can be synthesised in the following bullet points list and described in Fig. 2:

- Dense polygonal mesh model generation and detailed texturisation in Metashape;
- Mesh refinement in Metashape;
- Mesh Decimation, Retopology and Texture baking;
- Scene setup, controller input mapping, and mesh collider in Unity.

Dense Polygonal Mesh Model Generation and Detailed Texturisation in Metashape. Using photogrammetry, it is possible to create an extremely accurate model of real-world objects. Typically, a photogrammetric survey provides geometrically and radiometrically reliable data for documentation, modelling, simulation and analysis. Creating digital assets for VR using photogrammetry follows different requirements and constraints instead. Usually, in engineering, architecture, archaeology and geoscience, the mesh generation is a step that can be avoided, opting for the direct use of dense cloud as the basis for DEM and orthomosaic. In the case of digital assets for VR experiences, the dense polygonal mesh generation is mandatory and will be used to populate the scene.

Mesh Refinement in Metashape. The photo-consistent mesh refinement operation allows for iteratively recovering details (bas-relief or ditch) using a variational refinement method described in [51]. The result is a mesh that automatically and adaptively adjusts to image resolution. The required parameters are (i) quality, (ii) iterations and (iii) smoothness. The first defines the image downsizing with the same principle of image alignment; the second describes the number of iterations of the variational method; the third represents a classical smoothness threshold. Starting from the high-resolution polygonal mesh, the refined mesh is produced with an increased balance between noise suppression and feature recovery.

Mesh Decimation, Retopology and Texture Baking. The refined mesh obtained in the previous step is now the most detailed and optimised mesh obtainable from the photogrammetric workflow. Unfortunately, dense polygonal meshes are unsuitable and not remarkably manageable for VR software due to the data size and the complexity. Moreover, while most photogrammetric applications require only access to the 3D model and inspect it through viewer software, VR experiences require simulating a player moving closer to the object.

Therefore, it is common to produce several versions of the model, from low-poly to high-poly, interchanged during the user's movement. It is evident that creating several models of the same asset at different resolutions is a time-consuming process. Therefore, several methods have been developed to reshape the model, decreasing its size while keeping its complexity and details. These methods consist of reducing the number of polygons without losing details and maintaining the geometrical information of the original mesh. Mesh decimation and retopology methods are the most valuable methods to solve this task. In this work, both methods have been applied to evaluate which one allows the better result in terms of cost/benefits. Mesh decimation is utilised to diminish the complexity of a model by substituting a high-resolution mesh with a lower-resolution alternative while preserving the capability to represent the object's geometry accurately. Metashape software implements a specific tool that requires defining the target polygon number.

While Mesh Decimation applies a decimation algorithm to reduce the number of triangular faces, the Retopology method operates on a mesh's topology to obtain a cleaner and simplified polygonal mesh composed of more easily manageable shapes (usually quadrangular faces). This automatic technique is implemented in several software programs, which allows the conversion of the triangular mesh into a quad-mesh that guarantees an effective interaction with texturing and animation software, contributing to minimising the dimensions of the model and their rendering time. This conversion has been demanded by the Instant Meshes software [52].

Regardless of the method used to simplify the high-resolution mesh, the next step in the workflow is baking the diffusion maps and normal maps. Baking involves transferring the textures generated from the high-resolution model to all other low-poly models. This task requires consistency between the UV space of the texture and the 3D space of the model. Keeping as much quality as possible before the baking process is fundamental. Diffuse maps are texture maps that show the colour information reprojected by the images to the model. Normal maps complement diffuse maps and are texture maps that can give the appearance of additional geometry or details on flat surfaces and are used to make a low-poly mesh appear high-poly. Both maps are required to provide detailed material texture with depth perception.

In this workflow, we start by creating the high-resolution diffuse and normal texture in Metashape software. Then, we independently upload the quad-mesh or decimated mesh and bake the diffuse and normal maps. The procedure can be repeated for each Level of Detail designed for the VR experience.

Scene Setup, Controller Input Mapping, and Mesh Collider in Unity. Once all meshes are obtained in different LoD, converting them into scene-ready meshes with the correct orientation, pivot and uv set is required. This process can be done directly in Metashape during the export operations. The software chosen to develop the VR experience is Unity (references). The virtual set in Unity is called scene, and it hosts all the elements composing the project. A basic VR scene must contain an XR Origin, which defines the tracking data reference system. It allows the alignment of the tracking data acquired by the headset and aligned in a real-world reference system to the reference system defined in the unity environment. The XR Origin contains children's objects like the user's headset (Main Camera object) or the hand-held device (XR controller). Fundamental Objects are also the locomotion system to move around the scene and an input system to interact with the 3D objects. The test VR experience proposed in this work is a virtual tour without interaction of the portion of Turin city obtained with the integrated survey. Therefore, it was required to map the user's movement (walking, climbing) and to set up the mesh collider. Once the VR environment was correctly populated, the developed application was built and delivered for Android.

3 Results and Discussion

The results of the study conducted in this paper are shown and discussed in this chapter. Please refer to [44] for further information regarding the integrated survey, while the results regarding the integration of VR are described in an exhaustive manner. For illustrative purposes (also on a visual level) we have chosen to show the analyses regarding Carlo Alberto's statue.

3.1 Integrated Survey

The survey's final result consists of an integrated point cloud with about 5 billion points containing radiometric and LiDAR intensity information. The following checks were performed to validate the registration and georeferencing procedure accuracy concerning LiDAR and photogrammetric.

Concerning the LiDAR cloud, the accuracy of the scanning registering procedure was evaluated through the estimated deviations between the targets identified in the scans and their known coordinates (measured with the total station). The results of this analysis are shown in Table 3, and an RMSE of approximately 4 cm between points can be observed.

Table 3. Estimated residues between targets identified in scans and known coordinates [44].

	dX [m]	dY [m]	dZ [m]	Dist. [m]
Min	−0.08946	−0.07368	−0.13934	0.001692
Max	0.088073	0.105132	0.087002	0.156342
Mean	0.000671	−0.00033	0.002233	0.032446
RMSE	0.018788	0.020184	0.029044	0.040049

Concerning the photogrammetric survey, the final output was validated by analysing the estimated residuals on the control points and checkpoints (Table 4). The acquired measurements reflect the general geometric precision of the photogrammetric models produced using the Structure from Motion (SfM) technique. The point cloud comprehensively portrays the structures' rooftops and vertical dimensions. However, it lacks density in the lower sections of the buildings within narrow streets, where distortion is apparent even in oblique images. Consequently, a choice was made to reduce the quantity of ground-based photogrammetric data collection in these regions and instead utilise LiDAR data for 3D reconstruction.

Table 4. Results of the photogrammetric block adjustment [44].

	X (m)	Y (m)	Z (m)
RMSE	0.016	0.013	0.027
10 GCPs error	0.019	0.017	0.022
5 CPs error	0.016	0.013	0.027

It is important to remember that extraneous information is frequently captured during the data collection procedure. This issue is particularly pronounced in urban settings, where the raw scan data becomes distorted due to various interferences, such as highly reflective surfaces (like headlights and water), transparent materials (such as glass), and moving elements (for instance, people and vehicles). Among these factors, moving elements posed the most significant source of disturbance: pedestrians moving through the area during the measurement process led to disruptions in the point clouds. Initially, all individuals and unneeded objects within the scene were manually eliminated from the point cloud. Subsequently, the remaining noise was mitigated through the Statistical Outlier Removal (SOR) tool, which identifies and removes points likely unrelated to the modelled surfaces. This technique involves computing the average distance between each point and its neighbouring points (using six neighbours in this study). Points that exceed the average distance, multiplied by a coefficient derived from the standard deviation (0.5 in this instance), are filtered out. Despite these filtering procedures, managing the extensive point cloud still presented challenges and demanded substantial time due to its high point density. The point cloud was then systematically downsampled to facilitate the analysis and modelling tasks based on the area of interest.

3.2 VR Application

Among the seven portions processed in the previous section, Carlo Alberto's statue has been selected for the following parametrisation analysis. The dense point cloud obtained by the photogrammetric processing was a three-band 8-bit cloud composed of 47,405,562 points obtained by setting the quality parameter to "high", which downscale the images by a factor of 4. The processing time was 5 h and 32 min, producing a file of 706.05 MB. The dense cloud was used to compute the polygonal mesh model, obtaining 9,481,010 faces and 4,746,181 vertices in 3 h and 40 min. The vertices were colourised again with three bands of 8-unit colour information, and the entire mesh was texturised with a high-quality 8,192 × 8,192, 4 bands, uint8 texture. The obtained 3D mesh focused on achieving a high-quality level, maximising the number of triangles for optimal representation.

Fig. 5. Dense point cloud (left), dense triangulated mesh (middle) and textured model (right) of Carlo Alberto's statue.

Further processing steps have been applied in Metashape to obtain the mesh required for subsequent steps described in Fig. 5. Firstly, using the Metashape tool "refine mesh", an iterative process was used to recover surface details like bas-relief or ditch. Then, the texture was computed again on the refined model at the highest quality. The resulting 3D mesh was composed of 11,736,644 faces, 5,873,952 vertices and texturised with an $8,192 \times 8,192$, 4 bands, 8-unit image. The required processing time for refinement and texturing was 20 min, and the result was stored in 629.80 MB space. The result was exported both in.obj and in.ply file format, with the texture stored in.jpg (Fig. 6).

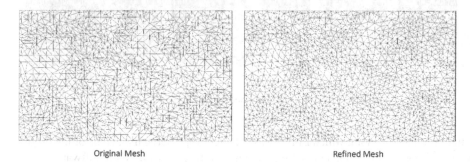

Fig. 6. Triangular Mesh structure: Original (left) and Refined (right).

Retopology. The refined 3D polygonal mesh model was imported into Instant Mesh software to perform an automatic retopology to minimise the model dimensions by transforming the mesh into a quadrangular faces model (Fig. 7). In the case of vertex singularities detected by the algorithm, a semi-automatic brush tool has been used to change the polygons' direction. Figure 8 shows different Levels of Details of the

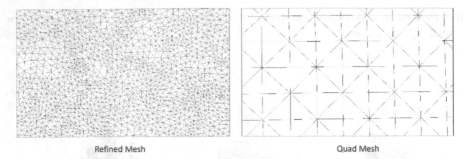

Refined Mesh   Quad Mesh

Fig. 7. Mesh obtained in Instant Mesh software at LoD 4.

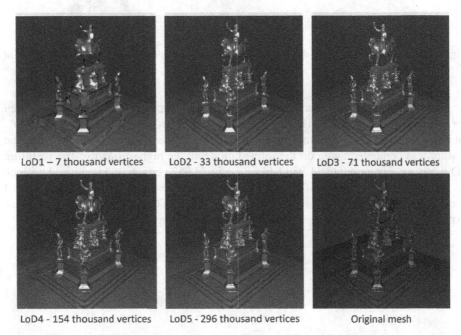

LoD1 – 7 thousand vertices   LoD2 - 33 thousand vertices   LoD3 - 71 thousand vertices

LoD4 - 154 thousand vertices   LoD5 - 296 thousand vertices   Original mesh

Fig. 8. Different LoD obtained in Instant Mesh software.

quadratic mesh, among which LoD 4 was selected to preserve the details of the original mesh, although obtaining a model light enough to be managed in VR software.

The normal map obtained in Metashape can now be applied to the low-poly model obtained by retopology. In VR software, this gives the appearance of fine surface details without the need for a high polygon count.

Unity. After setting up the VR scene, the controller input mapping and the mesh collider, the app was tested on the Meta Quest Pro device and the performance parameters were analysed. We used an XPS 15 7590 Windows 11 computer (Intel(R) Core(TM) i9-9980HK CPU @ 2.40 GHz, NVIDIA GeForce GTX 1650, 32 GB RAM) to run the VR experience and display it on a Meta Quest Pro (Model: DK94EC) through a wire connection (QuestLink) with a fresh rate of 90 Hz. These are reported in Table 5, while Fig. 9 shows an example of the interactive VR environment scene to explore Carlo Alberto's statue.

Table 5. Performance of the VR application.

Graphics	22.4 FPS
CPU:	Main 44.7 ms render thread 21.0 ms
Batches:	125
Tris:	1.3 M
Vert:	708.8k
Screen:	890 × 451–4.6 MB
SetPass calls:	125

Also, an entire scene of the integrated survey has been set up. The workflow followed was the same, but in order to maintain the optimal user experience, the Carigano Palace and the National Library were further divided in function of the floors. This resulted in generating a mesh with the maximum number of triangles for the lower portions of the facades while limiting the model's quality on the subsequent floors.

Fig. 9. VR environment scene of Carlo Alberto's statue and Palazzo Carignano.

4 Conclusions

In this work, we propose a comprehensive workflow for building a VR application using digital assets obtained by optimising photogrammetric and LiDAR 3D models. The workflow is applied on a high-detail, multi-scale 3D model of a city, which has been obtained through a multi-sensor integrated survey, exploiting UAV photogrammetry and TLS. VR is an innovative technology widely used to create faithful digital replicas of heritage sites and create immersive and engaging experiences. Historical city centres are also resistant to modification through the construction of modern infrastructure due to the presence of historical buildings and the opposition of many inner-city communities; therefore, VR applications can show how the construction of new infrastructure can change the neighbourhood's appearance while respecting the historical heritage. If in our previous study we limited ourselves to describing the data collection and processing phase in order to obtain a 3D model, in this study we also examined the precautions to be followed to implement this model correctly and efficiently in a virtual environment.

The importance of integrating geomatic techniques has emerged once again, and it will play a fundamental role in the following years since virtual reality is experiencing a quick increase of interest from private and public bodies for the innovative advertising and tourism of cultural heritage or museums. Optimising procedures to produce digital assets is fundamental to exploit the 3D survey potentiality without stressing headset hardware.

The results are excellent; however, further tests are needed to validate the proposed workflow in other environments (e.g., indoor, natural areas, etc.) and to describe and solve all the difficulties that may be encountered as the scenarios vary.

References

1. Klamer, A.: The value of cultural heritage. In: Hutter, M., Rizzo, I. (eds.) Economic Perspectives on Cultural Heritage, pp. 74–87. Palgrave Macmillan, London (1997). https://doi.org/10.1007/978-1-349-25824-6_5
2. Ogden, S.: Understanding, respect, and collaboration in cultural heritage preservation: a conservator's developing perspective. Libr. Trends **56**, 275–287 (2007). https://doi.org/10.1353/lib.2007.0056
3. Lussetyowati, T.: Preservation and conservation through cultural heritage tourism. case study: Musi Riverside Palembang. Procedia Soc. Behav. Sci. **184**, 401–406 (2015). https://doi.org/10.1016/j.sbspro.2015.05.109
4. Araoz, G.F.: Preserving heritage places under a new paradigm. J. Cult. Herit. Manag. Sustain. Dev. **1**, 55–60 (2011). https://doi.org/10.1108/20441261111129933
5. Gaitatzes, A., Christopoulos, D., Roussou, M.: Reviving the past: cultural heritage meets virtual reality. In: Proceedings of the 2001 Conference on Virtual Reality, Archeology, and Cultural Heritage, pp. 103–110. ACM, Glyfada (2001). https://doi.org/10.1145/584993.585011
6. Bekele, M.K., Pierdicca, R., Frontoni, E., Malinverni, E.S., Gain, J.: A survey of augmented, virtual, and mixed reality for cultural heritage. J. Comput. Cult. Herit. **11**, 1–36 (2018). https://doi.org/10.1145/3145534
7. Skublewska-Paszkowska, M., Milosz, M., Powroznik, P., Lukasik, E.: 3D technologies for intangible cultural heritage preservation—literature review for selected databases. Herit. Sci. **10**, 3 (2022). https://doi.org/10.1186/s40494-021-00633-x
8. Cantatore, E., Lasorella, M., Fatiguso, F.: Virtual reality to support technical knowledge in cultural heritage. The case study of cryptoporticus in the archaeological site of Egnatia (Italy). Int. Arch. Photogramm. Remote Sens. Spatial Inf. Sci. XLIV-M-1-2020, 465–472 (2020). https://doi.org/10.5194/isprs-archives-XLIV-M-1-2020-465-2020

9. Younes, G., et al.: Virtual and augmented reality for rich interaction with cultural heritage sites: a case study from the Roman Theater at Byblos. Digit. Appl. Archaeol. Cult. Herit. **5**, 1–9 (2017). https://doi.org/10.1016/j.daach.2017.03.002
10. Canciani, M., Conigliaro, E., Del Grasso, M., Papalini, P., Saccone, M.: 3D survey and augmented reality for cultural heritage. The case study of Aurelian Wall at Castra Praetoria in Rome. Int. Arch. Photogramm. Remote Sens. Spatial Inf. Sci. **XLI-B5**, 931–937 (2016). https://doi.org/10.5194/isprs-archives-XLI-B5-931-2016
11. Economou, T., Vosinakis, S.: Mobile augmented reality games as an engaging tool for cultural heritage dissemination: a case study. (2018). https://doi.org/10.5281/ZENODO.1214569
12. Valtolina, S., Franzoni, S., Mazzoleni, P., Bertino, E.: Dissemination of cultural heritage content through virtual reality and multimedia techniques: a case study. In: 11th International Multimedia Modelling Conference, pp. 214–221. IEEE, Honolulu (2005). https://doi.org/10.1109/MMMC.2005.36
13. Mortara, M., Catalano, C.E., Bellotti, F., Fiucci, G., Houry-Panchetti, M., Petridis, P.: Learning cultural heritage by serious games. J. Cult. Herit. **15**, 318–325 (2014). https://doi.org/10.1016/j.culher.2013.04.004
14. Sun, Q., Wei, L.-Y., Kaufman, A.: Mapping virtual and physical reality. ACM Trans. Graph. **35**, 1–12 (2016). https://doi.org/10.1145/2897824.2925883
15. LaValle, S.M.: Virtual Reality. Cambridge University Press, Oxford (2023)
16. Bowman, D.A., McMahan, R.P.: Virtual reality: how much immersion is enough? Computer **40**, 36–43 (2007). https://doi.org/10.1109/MC.2007.257
17. Pensieri, C., Pennacchini, M.: Overview: virtual reality in medicine. JVWR **7** (2014). https://doi.org/10.4101/jvwr.v7i1.6364
18. Riener, R., Harders, M.: Introduction to virtual reality in medicine. In: Virtual Reality in Medicine, pp. 1–12. Springer, London (2012). https://doi.org/10.1007/978-1-4471-4011-5_1
19. Li, L., et al.: Application of virtual reality technology in clinical medicine. Am. J. Transl. Res. **9**, 3867–3880 (2017)
20. McCloy, R., Stone, R.: Science, medicine, and the future: virtual reality in surgery. BMJ **323**, 912–915 (2001). https://doi.org/10.1136/bmj.323.7318.912
21. Liu, X., Zhang, J., Hou, G., Wang, Z.: Virtual reality and its application in military. IOP Conf. Ser. Earth Environ. Sci. **170**, 032155 (2018). https://doi.org/10.1088/1755-1315/170/3/032155
22. Tzanavari, A., Tsapatsoulis, N. (eds.) Affective, Interactive and Cognitive Methods for E-Learning Design: Creating an Optimal Education Experience. IGI Global (2010). https://doi.org/10.4018/978-1-60566-940-3
23. Häkkilä, J., et al.: Visiting a virtual graveyard: designing virtual reality cultural heritage experiences. In: Proceedings of the 18th International Conference on Mobile and Ubiquitous Multimedia, pp. 1–4. ACM, Pisa (2019). https://doi.org/10.1145/3365610.3368425
24. Donghui, C., Guanfa, L., Wensheng, Z., Qiyuan, L., Shuping, B., Xiaokang, L.: Virtual reality technology applied in digitalization of cultural heritage. Cluster Comput. **22**, 10063–10074 (2019). https://doi.org/10.1007/s10586-017-1071-5
25. Giangreco, I., et al.: VIRTUE: a virtual reality museum Experience. In: Proceedings of the 24th International Conference on Intelligent User Interfaces: Companion, pp. 119–120. ACM, Marina del Ray (2019). https://doi.org/10.1145/3308557.3308706
26. Lee, H., Jung, T.H., Tom Dieck, M.C., Chung, N.: Experiencing immersive virtual reality in museums. Inf. Manage. **57**, 103229 (2020). https://doi.org/10.1016/j.im.2019.103229
27. Vincke, S., De Lima Hernandez, R., Bassier, M., Vergauwen, M.: Immersive visualisation of construction site point cloud data, meshes and Bim models in a VR environment using a gaming engine. Int. Arch. Photogramm. Remote Sens. Spatial Inf. Sci. **XLII-5/W2**, 77–83 (2019). https://doi.org/10.5194/isprs-archives-XLII-5-W2-77-2019

28. Dhanda, A., et al.: Recreating cultural heritage environments for VR using photogrammetry. Int. Arch. Photogramm. Remote Sens. Spatial Inf. Sci. **XLII-2/W9**, 305–310 (2019). https://doi.org/10.5194/isprs-archives-XLII-2-W9-305-2019

29. Mikhail, E.M., Bethel, J.S., McGlone, J.C.: Introduction to Modern Photogrammetry. Wiley, New York (2001)

30. Zhao, S., Kang, F., Li, J.: Concrete dam damage detection and localisation based on YOLOv5s-HSC and photogrammetric 3D reconstruction. Autom. Constr. **143**, 104555 (2022). https://doi.org/10.1016/j.autcon.2022.104555

31. Maas, H.-G., Hampel, U.: Photogrammetric techniques in civil engineering material testing and structure monitoring. Photogramm. Eng. Remote Sens. **72**, 39–45 (2006). https://doi.org/10.14358/PERS.72.1.39

32. Bemis, S.P., et al.: Ground-based and UAV-Based photogrammetry: a multi-scale, high-resolution mapping tool for structural geology and paleoseismology. J. Struct. Geol. **69**, 163–178 (2014). https://doi.org/10.1016/j.jsg.2014.10.007

33. Remondino, F., El-Hakim, S.: Image-based 3D Modelling: a review: image-based 3D modelling: a review. Photogram. Rec. **21**, 269–291 (2006). https://doi.org/10.1111/j.1477-9730.2006.00383.x

34. Kwiatek, K., Tokarczyk, R.: Immersive photogrammetry in 3D modelling: Fotogrametria immersyjna w modelowaniu 3D. Geom. **9**, 51 (2015). https://doi.org/10.7494/geom.2015.9.2.51

35. Singh, S.P., Jain, K., Mandla, V.R.: Virtual 3D city modeling: techniques and applications. Int. Arch. Photogramm. Remote Sens. Spatial Inf. Sci. **XL-2/W2**, 73–91 (2013). https://doi.org/10.5194/isprsarchives-XL-2-W2-73-2013

36. Zhu, Q., Hu, M., Zhang, Y., Du, Z.: Research and practice in three-dimensional city modeling. Geo-spat. Inf. Sci. **12**, 18–24 (2009). https://doi.org/10.1007/s11806-009-0195-z

37. Sato, T., Kanbara, M., Yokoya, N.: Outdoor scene reconstruction from multiple image sequences captured by a hand-held video camera. In: Proceedings of IEEE International Conference on Multisensor Fusion and Integration for Intelligent Systems, MFI2003, pp. 113–118. IEEE, Tokyo (2003). https://doi.org/10.1109/MFI-2003.2003.1232642

38. Pepe, M., Fregonese, L., Crocetto, N.: Use of SfM-MVS approach to nadir and oblique images generated through aerial cameras to build 2.5D map and 3D models in urban areas. Geocarto Int. **37**, 120–141 (2022). https://doi.org/10.1080/10106049.2019.1700558

39. Smith, M.W., Carrivick, J.L., Quincey, D.J.: Structure from motion photogrammetry in physical geography. Progr. Phys. Geogr. Earth Environ. **40**, 247–275 (2016). https://doi.org/10.1177/0309133315615805

40. Tse, R.O.C., Gold, C., Kidner, D.: 3D city modelling from LIDAR data. In: van Oosterom, P., Zlatanova, S., Penninga, F., Fendel, E.M. (eds.) Advances in 3D Geoinformation Systems, pp. 161–175. Springer, Heidelberg (2008). https://doi.org/10.1007/978-3-540-72135-2_10

41. Wang, C., Wen, C., Dai, Y., Yu, S., Liu, M.: Urban 3D modeling with mobile laser scanning: a review. Virt. Real. Intell. Hardw. **2**, 175–212 (2020). https://doi.org/10.1016/j.vrih.2020.05.003

42. Ramos, M.M., Remondino, F.: Data fusion in Cultural Heritage – a review. Int. Arch. Photogramm. Remote Sens. Spatial Inf. Sci. **XL-5/W7**, 359–363 (2015). https://doi.org/10.5194/isprsarchives-XL-5-W7-359-2015

43. Sahin, C., Alkis, A., Ergun, B., Kulur, S., Batuk, F., Kilic, A.: Producing 3D city model with the combined photogrammetric and laser scanner data in the example of Taksim Cumhuriyet square. Opt. Lasers Eng. **50**, 1844–1853 (2012). https://doi.org/10.1016/j.optlaseng.2012.05.019

44. Grasso, N., Spadavecchia, C., Di Pietra, V., Belcore, E.: LiDAR and SfM-MVS integrated approach to build a highly detailed 3D virtual model of urban areas: In: Proceedings of the

9th International Conference on Geographical Information Systems Theory, Applications and Management, pp. 128–135. SCITEPRESS - Science and Technology Publications, Praguec (2023). https://doi.org/10.5220/0011760800003473

45. Chang, E., Seo, D., Kim, H.T., Yoo, B.: An integrated model of cybersickness: understanding user's discomfort in virtual reality. JOK **45**, 251–279 (2018). https://doi.org/10.5626/JOK. 2018.45.3.251

46. Zhdanov, A.D., Zhdanov, D.D., Bogdanov, N.N., Potemin, I.S., Galaktionov, V.A., Sorokin, M.I.: Discomfort of visual perception in virtual and mixed reality systems. Program. Comput. Soft. **45**, 147–155 (2019). https://doi.org/10.1134/S036176881904011X

47. Obradović, M., Vasiljević, I., Đurić, I., Kićanović, J., Stojaković, V., Obradović, R.: Virtual reality models based on photogrammetric surveys—a case study of the iconostasis of the Serbian orthodox Cathedral Church of Saint Nicholas in Sremski Karlovci (Serbia). Appl. Sci. **10**, 2743 (2020). https://doi.org/10.3390/app10082743

48. Portalés, C., Lerma, J.L., Pérez, C.: Photogrammetry and augmented reality for cultural heritage applications. Photogramm. Rec. **24**, 316–331 (2009). https://doi.org/10.1111/j.1477-9730.2009.00549.x

49. Hilfert, T., König, M.: Low-cost virtual reality environment for engineering and construction. Vis. Eng. **4**, 2 (2016). https://doi.org/10.1186/s40327-015-0031-5

50. Placitelli, A.P., Gallo, L.: Low-cost augmented reality systems via 3D point cloud sensors. In: 2011 Seventh International Conference on Signal Image Technology & Internet-Based Systems, pp. 188–192. IEEE, Dijon (2011). https://doi.org/10.1109/SITIS.2011.43

51. Vu, H., Keriven, R., Labatut, P., Pons, J.-P.: Towards high-resolution large-scale multi-view stereo. In: Proceedings of the IEEE Conference on CVPR 2009, pp. 1430–1437 (2009)

52. Jakob, W., Tarini, M., Panozzo, D., Sorkine-Hornung, O.: Instant field-aligned meshes. ACM Trans. Graph. **34**, 1–15 (2015). https://doi.org/10.1145/2816795.2818078

Dynamic Real-Time Spatio-Temporal Acquisition and Rendering in Adverse Environments

Somnath Dutta⊙, Fabio Ganovelli$^{(\boxtimes)}$⊙, and Paolo Cignoni⊙

Institute of Information Science and Technologies, "Alessandro Faedo" (ISTI), Italian National Research Council (CNR), Via Giuseppe Moruzzi 1, 56124 Pisa, Italy
{somnath.dutta,fabio.ganovelli,paolo.cignoni}@isti.cnr.it

Abstract. This paper introduces NausicaaVR, a novel hardware/software system designed to acquire and render intricate 3D environments, with a particular emphasis on challenging and adverse contexts. In doing so, we navigate the complex landscape of system calibration and rendering, while seamlessly integrating data from multiple sensors. We explore the distinctive challenges inherent in adverse environments, juxtaposing them against conventional automotive scenarios. Through a comprehensive exposition of all constituent elements of the NausicaaVR system, we offer transparent insights into the encountered obstacles and the intricate decisions that were instrumental in surmounting them. This study seeks to illuminate the developmental trajectory of NausicaaVR and analogous systems, thereby furnishing a repository of knowledge and understanding poised to benefit future research and the pragmatic implementation of such cutting-edge technologies.

Keywords: Multi-sensor calibration · Real-time rendering · Virtual reality

1 Introduction

In a multi-sensor environment, perception and rendering play crucial roles in understanding and representing the surrounding world. With the advancements in sensor technologies, such as cameras, lidar, radar, and depth sensors, the ability to capture rich and diverse data about the environment has greatly expanded. Multi-sensor perception involves the integration and fusion of data from multiple sensors to generate a comprehensive understanding of the scene, including the detection and tracking of objects, estimation of their poses and velocities, and the creation of detailed 3D models. On the other hand, rendering in a multi-sensor environment aims to create realistic and immersive visual representations of the perceived scene, taking into account the different sensor modalities and their respective characteristics. This involves techniques such as sensor fusion, data alignment, mapping, and rendering algorithms to generate accurate and visually appealing virtual representations of the environment. The combination of multi-sensor perception and rendering enables applications in various domains,

---

NAUSICAA- NAUtical Safety by means of Integrated ComputerAssisted Appliances 4.0 (DIT.AD004.136).

C. Grueau et al. (Eds.): GISTAM 2023, CCIS 2107, pp. 34–53, 2024.
https://doi.org/10.1007/978-3-031-60277-1_3

including autonomous driving [6], virtual reality, augmented reality, and robotics, where an accurate understanding and realistic visualization of the environment are paramount.

Multi-sensor perception and rendering pose several challenges due to the complexity of integrating data from multiple sensors and synthesizing a coherent representation of the environment. Some of the key Challenges include:

- **Data Fusion.** Combining data from different sensors with varying characteristics. The challenge lies in aligning and synchronizing the data streams, handling differences in resolution, accuracy, and noise levels, and resolving conflicts or inconsistencies between sensor measurements.
- **Sensor Calibration**: Accurate calibration of sensors is essential for achieving reliable multi-sensor perception. Ensuring that the sensors are properly aligned, calibrated, and synchronized is a non-trivial task. Sensor calibration involves estimating intrinsic and extrinsic parameters, such as camera intrinsics, lidar calibration, and sensor-to-sensor transformations.
- **Occlusion and Sensor Limitations.** Dealing with occlusions and handling sensor limitations are important challenges in multi-sensor perception. Occlusions can lead to missing or incomplete data, requiring techniques to infer or reconstruct occluded regions. Moreover, sensor limitations, such as limited field of view, range, or resolution, need to be considered to ensure accurate perception and rendering of the environment.
- **Real-time Performance.** Multi-sensor perception and rendering systems often operate in real-time applications such as robotics, autonomous vehicles, or augmented reality. Achieving real-time performance while maintaining accuracy and reliability is a challenge. Efficient algorithms, optimization strategies, and hardware acceleration are necessary to meet the stringent timing requirements.

With the above-mentioned objective in focus, we highlight the substantial outcomes of our work as summarized below.

- a testbed architecture with multiple cameras and low-cost lidar sensors, described in Sect. 3.1
- an ad hoc method (Sect. 4) for registration of input data in a common reference frame

The paper is organized into multiple sections focusing on related works in Sect. 2, a description of the overall system-cum-architecture in Sect. 3 followed by calibration of lidars and cameras in Sect. 4.

2   Related Work

In this section, we aim to provide a comprehensive overview of existing literature, primarily focusing on two key aspects: the system framework and the spatio-temporal calibration of a multi-modal sensor system. Regarding the system framework, we will explore previous works that have proposed various architectures, designs, or methodologies for integrating multiple sensors within a cohesive system. This includes studies that have investigated the fusion of data from different modalities, the synchronization of sensor outputs, or the development of algorithms for real-time processing and analysis.

Additionally, we will delve into the topic of spatio-temporal calibration in multimodal sensor systems. This area of research deals with the alignment and synchronization of spatial and temporal data captured by different sensors. We will examine different calibration techniques and algorithms proposed in the literature, along with their advantages, limitations, and potential applications.

System-Framework. Visual sensors are essential components in maneuvering operations across diverse scenarios, such as street navigation with automotive vehicles [19], aerial navigation with drones [26], and marine operations in boats and ships [17]. In recent years, rapid advancements in technologies such as sensing devices, Artificial Intelligence (AI), and the Internet of Things (IoT) have sparked significant transformations across various domains, leading to their widespread adoption in diverse applications. Tonnis et al. [41] emphasized the increasing significance of spatial sensor systems in cars, forming the basis for safety and driver assistance systems. The authors present their developed visualization system for spatial sensor data, incorporating various setups and visualization devices to ensure precise spatial alignment and support the advancement of driver assistance systems. Vu et al. [42] presented a multi-sensor-based approach for object perception in automotive applications, addressing the detection, tracking, and classification of objects while considering various classes. The proposed method employs fusion techniques to combine information from lidar and camera sensors, resulting in a more reliable representation of detected objects in real-life scenarios.

Our literature research also revolves around marine maneuver and navigation, aligning with our research project on a similar topic. However, our framework takes a more generic approach, designed to accommodate variability with necessary modifications. In the field of marine vessels, there has been active research and development of technology-related autonomous ships [13,36] to enhance safety by mitigating human errors and improving working conditions through reduced crew workload. One noteworthy application-oriented research and development project is SmartKai [8], which is centered around creating a parking system for ships at the harbor, employing lidar sensors. The project includes the development of a smart user interface, enabling ship crews to effortlessly visualize navigation data across various display platforms. Moreover, in a study by [37], a camera-based visual sensing system is proposed to cater to maritime navigation and reconnaissance applications, including obstacle avoidance and area survey analysis.

Ruessmeier et al. [34] conceptualized and implemented an experimental maritime testbed for sensor data fusion, communication technology, and data stream analysis tools. The setup is highly flexible and applicable in various research fields, including e-navigation and situational awareness generation. Brinkmann et al. [3] introduced LAB-SKAUS, a maritime physical testbed/cyber-physical system, offering maritime-specific components like a reference waterway, research boat, and mobile bridge. The proposed architecture includes a data model, message parser, wireless infrastructure, and a polymorphic interface, enabling the integration of various prototype designs within LAB-SKAUS. [21] discuss digitalization in marine vessels as a significant process directed toward autonomous navigation, cost reduction, safety, and reliability. The authors point out that the complete system consisting of advanced sensors, Artificial Intelligence, and alternative display techniques (VR, AR) is a major requirement in the marine intelligence system, but also pitches an enormous challenge for integration and deployment. [29] proposed a simple hardware system and software architecture for collecting the sensor data (non-visual) targeting autonomous surface vessels (ASVs). Furthermore, a human-machine interface (HMI) is implemented as part of the system.

A chronological trend of the ASV's existing autonomy levels in marine vessels and multi-agent control architecture from the perspective of ASVs is presented in [35]. According to the authors, situation awareness that forms an integral block of the navigation systems heavily relies on sensor fusion and the corresponding data visualization. [38] presents a detailed review of the sensor and AI technique for environment perception and awareness for autonomous ships. [43] explores the use of AI techniques to integrate multiple sensor modalities into a cohesive approach for autonomous ship navigation. The use of multiple redundant sensors overcomes the limitations and vulnerabilities of the individual sensor and the usage of advanced learning methodology addresses key areas of detection and identification providing comprehensive situational awareness to be effective in real-time maneuvering.

Multi-Sensor Calibration. In order to effectively integrate information (spatially and temporally) obtained from multiple sensing modalities, it is essential to represent them in a common reference frame. The problem of estimation of the rigid body transformation between the multimodal sensory information (camera and LiDAR) has been extensively studied in the past two decades [16,22,30]. Despite recent developments, fusing multimodal sensory information is still a challenging problem [33]. [23] proposed a framework tailored for global-shutter camera and 3D LiDAR setups with fixed internal camera calibration parameters and an unknown but constant time offset between the sensors. Kodaira et al. [18] proposed a segmentation-based framework to jointly estimate geometric and temporal parameters for calibrating a camera-LIDAR sensor suite, achieving accurate real-time calibration without the need for calibration labels. The primary limitation lies in its dependency on high-quality semantic segmentation masks, which may impact calibration accuracy, particularly in scenarios with compromised segmentation performance. Grammatikopoulos et al. [12] presented a straightforward method to calibrate Lidar-camera systems using AprilTag markers and a custom retroreflective target. The approach achieves geometric alignment and temporal synchronization, demonstrated on a four-camera mobile mapping system with integrated Velodyne Lidar for accurate multi-camera point cloud texturing. A trihedral object's geometric constraint is employed to achieve a calibration through nonlinear square optimization of a 3D lidar-camera system in [11]. While the method does rely on minimal manual input, it's important to note that in scenarios involving irregular or complex environments, the trihedral assumption may not remain valid. In such cases, the method's performance could decline, particularly if the initial plane region inputs are significantly inaccurate. The research from [27] addresses the limitations of traditional calibration methods by introducing a novel targetless, structureless approach for spatio-temporal alignment between LiDAR and visible cameras on robotic systems. Unlike methods assuming scene geometry, this approach accommodates various sensor configurations and environmental conditions, showcasing accuracy in estimating spatio-temporal parameters.

This paper extends the work presented in [9] introduces a comprehensive framework centered around affordable sensors. In contrast to existing methodologies, our approach inherently tackles the challenge of registering and calibrating multi-modal data. This is particularly crucial given the issues of low resolution, lidar data sparsity, and complex environmental conditions. We provide detailed insights into the alignment of multi-modal data in Sect. 4, carefully considering the aforementioned challenges. This is achieved through a combination of tailored calibration objects and a streamlined algorithmic approach. Importantly, we propose a calibration refinement procedure based on the photo-consistency model as elaborated in Sect. 4.3 that reduces the overall calibration errors and ghosting artifacts induced by asynchronous data collection.

3 NausicaaVR-Framework

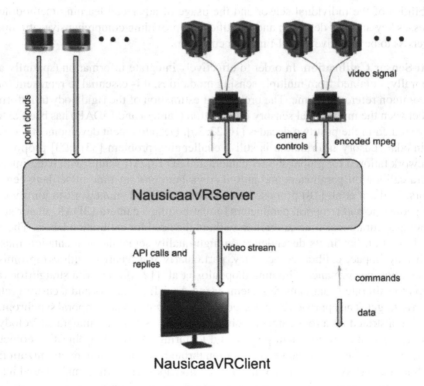

Fig. 1. Hardware-Software System (from [9]).

The schematic diagram 1 offers a holistic view of our entire framework. Subsequent sections provide in-depth elucidation of our framework, encompassing the hardware configuration in Sect. 3.1 and the proprietary software interface Sect. 3.2.

Our hardware configuration entails a multi-modal sensor system integrating two Lidar scanners and four embedded color cameras, each equipped with fish-eye lenses.

To be precise, we employ Velodyne's VLP-16 PUCK LITE lidar scanners and Imaging Source cameras [14], which are purpose-built for operating effectively in demanding environmental conditions.

3.1 Sensor System Configuration

The cameras as shown in Fig. 1 are interfaced with NVIDIA Jetson embedded hardware [25], running on the Linux Tegra OS. NVIDIA's Jetson hardware and its extensive software development kits (SDKs) also cater to Artificial Intelligence (AI) applications, rendering them exceptionally well-suited for autonomous machines and integrated systems. The captured video signals from the cameras undergo H264 encoding, facilitating efficient transmission of the resulting streams over a wired network to the server.

With the hardware acceleration capabilities of Jetson, the video stream is rapidly encoded, enabling seamless transmission of HD-resolution data at 60 fps. The parameters of each individual camera sensor are optimally refined through a manual process, leveraging information from the camera software development kit (SDK) and tailored to suit the specific acquisition environment. Moreover, the H264 encoding and streaming parameters are fine-tuned to capitalize on the hardware encoding acceleration capabilities offered by Nvidia Jetson. These carefully calibrated camera sensor data and encoding parameters are seamlessly integrated using the GStreamer open-source multimedia framework pipeline, enabling efficient data transmission as UDP packets.

Concurrently, the individual lidars (VLP-16) proficiently stream real-time 3D point data as UDP packets via ethernet. Subsequently, an Intel core-i9 PC, complemented with a powerful Nvidia GeForce RTX 3090 graphics card (24 GB) and running on the Windows 11 Platform, is designated to receive UDP packets from each sensor for further processing and visualization. This setup enables the system to execute data processing tasks with utmost precision and present a comprehensive visualization of the acquired data.

3.2 Software Configuration

The data that streams from both the lidars and cameras undergoes further processing and visualization through our proprietary application framework. This framework serves as a robust platform primarily dedicated to the real-time rendering of lidar point clouds and the visualization of camera streams. Importantly, it facilitates alignment operations for both lidar-lidar and camera-lidar data, a crucial step that enables us to effectively map the geometric data extracted from the 3D point cloud and the visual texture information derived from the camera images. This intricate process culminates in the creation of a realistic rendered view of the environment. Moreover, our framework extends its capabilities to encompass remote visualization, achieved through MJPEG streaming accessible via standard web browsers. This feature enables users to remotely view the rendered data without the need for specialized software. Crucially, the framework establishes a seamless communication channel between client applications and the Server PC. This interaction is made possible through the utilization of network socket connections and advanced API functionalities. This sophisticated communication mechanism empowers clients to actively engage with the application hosted on the server PC. It allows clients to virtually explore the scene from various camera viewpoints, providing them with a dynamic and interactive experience. Furthermore, the system facilitates the reception of essential feedback, enhancing the interactivity and usefulness of the application.

4   Spatio-Temporal Registration of LIDARs and RGB Cameras

The calibration challenge involving Velodyne VLP16 is widely acknowledged in the literature, as evident from studies like [1, 20, 28]. This challenge primarily revolves around establishing 3D-2D correspondences between the LIDAR-generated point cloud and RGB camera images. The complexity of this task is influenced by several factors:

- **LIDAR Resolution.** Determining the 3D position of a target point from a point cloud relies on inferred information. Sparse point clouds pose more difficulty in locating target points accurately. The more the latter is sparse, the more difficult it is to find the target point.
- **Sensor Disposition.** Since the target points need to be seen both from the LIDAR and the camera, their relative position influences the sparsity of the point cloud. As an example, in practical scenarios where the camera is typically situated at a distance from the LIDAR and faces away from it, the sampling on the target will be less dense.
- **Environment Conditions.** In a controlled environment where LIDARs and cameras are present, we have the flexibility to create customized configurations that simplify the process of finding correspondences. As an illustration, within an empty room, we could utilize the corner points located at the juncture of walls and either the floor or ceiling.

The challenges in our particular scenario include all the aforementioned factors. The VLP16's limited vertical axis resolution and depth precision contribute to the intricacy. Additionally, the spatial separation between cameras and LIDARs compounds the issue, often placing them at considerable distances. Furthermore, the need for calibration in adverse environments, such as on a boat over water, exacerbates the difficulties due to the lack of reference points. Given the intricacies posed by these factors, our strategy entailed the development of a custom-designed target. This target strikes a balance between portability and visibility at a distance, as elaborated in the following section.

4.1   Calibration Target Design

We aimed to create a tangible target that could be consistently and automatically detected in both point clouds and images. Simultaneously, it needed to be simple to construct and lightweight to be usable with commercial drones. The initial prototype took the form of a cusp, formed by the intersection of three non-coplanar planar cardboard pieces (depicted in Fig. 2, left). A similar approach was proposed in [4]. This design choice was based on the principle that even incomplete sampling of the three planar regions would establish their supporting planes and consequently the cusp point (the intersection of these planes). However, although this method functioned to some extent, we observed that the accuracy of the detected cusp point was compromised even at relatively short distances. This inaccuracy stemmed from the precision of LIDAR values, whereby fitting planes to a relatively small spatial region (approximately 100 points) could lead to multiple equally valid fitting planes due to the granularity of measurements. As a result, the intersection of these planes defined a point with a radius spanning several centimeters even when positioned just 3 m from the LIDAR.

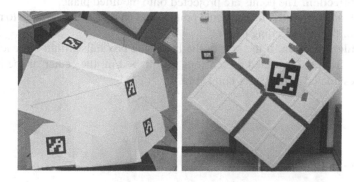

Fig. 2. Left: preliminary version of the target; Right: refined target used with our system (from [9]).

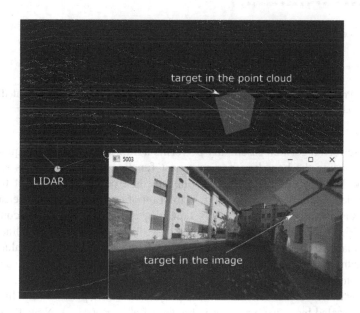

Fig. 3. Example of how the target appears in the point cloud and in one of the RGB images (from [9]).

Our designed target strategically leverages the LIDAR's most precise scan directions, particularly the azimuthal direction, while remaining robust against issues like vertical low-frequency sampling and potential depth measurement inaccuracies. The approach involves employing a straightforward $1\,m \times 1\,m$ square suspended from one corner, with its center serving as the target point (as illustrated on the right side of Fig. 2). An example of the resulting point cloud is shown in Fig. 3. The subsequent procedure involves the following steps:

1. **Fitting a Plane.** A plane is fitted using the sampling points of the square.
2. **Point Projection.** The points are projected onto the fitted plane.
3. **Point Cloud Rotation.** The projected point cloud on the plane is rotated to minimize the size of the 2D bounding box.
4. **Target Identification.** If the size of the bounding box falls within a predetermined tolerance from the expected dimensions of $1\,m \times 1\,m$, the center of the bounding box is designated as the target point (Fig. 4).

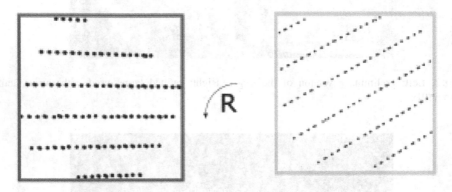

Fig. 4. Left: Points on the target projected on their fitting plane. Right: Point rotated to fit the (known) bounding box of the target (from [9]).

The described algorithm essentially performs a fitting of a fixed-size square on the point cloud, using the bounding box as a cost function. Note that, in its simplicity, this method has two useful qualities. It only needs a partial sampling of the points along the sides in order to be detected. It is tolerant of errors in in-depth measurement. This latter statement can be supported by sketching a simple proof. Let us consider the scheme in Fig. 5 showing the 2-dimensional case. The actual supporting line (that is, the actual plane of the target) is L but because of the imprecise depth values, we fit the point with line L_f. Let h be the thickness of the slab of points that are supposed to be on the same line. We can find the angle between the worst fitting line L_F and L as $\alpha_{err} = arctan(h/0.5)$. It follows that the projection of the point on this line will be erroneously scaled by $cos(\alpha_e rr)$, that is $\|p_f\| = \|p\| * cos(\alpha_{err})$. Now, to put things in perspective, consider that at 4 m from the LIDAR, we can have a depth error around $0.03\,m$, which gives an error of $cos(arctan(0.03/0.5)) = 0.998$, which means that we can have the square shrunk at most by 2 mm.

Detecting the same target in the RGB images is an easier problem which is solved with consolidated markers such as the Aruco markers [10].

4.2   Calibration Procedure

The calibration process involves showing the target to the LIDARs and cameras until an adequate number of correspondences are accumulated for data alignment. During initialization, the user is prompted to indicate the point cloud region containing the target through a straightforward mouse click. Subsequently, continuous tracking of the target within the point clouds is established.

Whenever the target is identified in both point clouds, a fresh 3D-3D correspondence is gathered and used for point cloud alignment. Should the target be located in at least one point cloud, its corresponding 2D point in the images is sought. This leads to the creation of a 3D-2D correspondence for each image where the target point is located.

In theory, just four 3D-3D correspondences are required for point cloud alignment, and the same number of 3D-2D correspondences are needed for each image. However, the alignment's efficacy is heavily reliant on the precision and distribution of these correspondences. For instance, nearly quasi-collinear 3D points can yield unstable point cloud alignment, while 2D points concentrated within a small image area may result in inaccuracies. As such, the aforementioned simple algorithm necessitates further elaboration to accommodate these intricacies.

Acquisition Time. Given that our data is collected from various sources asynchronously, ensuring their simultaneous acquisition is not feasible, and often not the case. This becomes particularly problematic when the target is in motion, as it can lead to erroneous correspondences.

To address this challenge, we determine the target's speed and utilize its position only when it exhibits extremely slow movement (e.g., 5 cm/s in our tests). Furthermore, we evaluate the timestamps of point clouds and associated data, discarding correspondences if the time interval between the point cloud and the corresponding images surpasses a predefined threshold (e.g., 100 ms in our experiments). These strategies

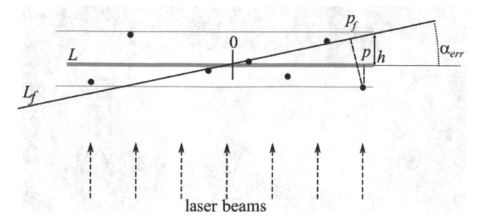

Fig. 5. Proof sketch that approximated depth measurement has limited effect on the computation of the target size (from [9]).

Fig. 6. All the correspondences found between the image and the 3D geometry as red dots. Selected correspondences are rendered with blue circles. The greyscale version of the image is rendered in order to better highlight the correspondence points (from [9] (Color figure online)).

are implemented to mitigate the impact of asynchronous data acquisition from various sources.

Distribution of Correspondences. For both 3D-3D and 3D-2D alignments, it is imperative to possess a sparse set of correspondences. Additionally, these correspondences should avoid configurations that could lead to degeneracy, such as collinear points (for

Fig. 7. Two images that overlap imprecisely create the illusion of fuzzy discontinuities, like at the frame of the blue doors in the image. (Color figure online)

both types of alignments) or 3D points residing on a single plane (specifically for 3D-2D alignment).

To achieve this, we leverage the progressive Poisson Sampling technique [7]. Commencing with an initially large disk radius R, we search for four samples that maintain a minimum separation of R units. If these samples satisfy the non-degeneracy criteria, the process is successful. If not, we reduce R by one-tenth and repeat the procedure until a suitable set of samples is obtained or until the process fails. Figure 6 visually depicts an instance of point selection within one of the RGB frames using this method.

4.3 Calibration Refinement

As previously mentioned, the asynchronous collection of point clouds and images can adversely affect the quality of the calibration procedure by providing imprecise 3D-2D correspondences. This, in turn, leads to the occurrence of ghosting artifacts, which become apparent when multiple images of the same geometry are not precisely aligned (Fig. 7 illustrates an example). To enhance the accuracy of the registration process and minimize these ghosting artifacts, we propose an output-sensitive procedure.

Our algorithm operates in pairs. It designates one camera as the reference and adjusts the extrinsic parameters of the other camera (i.e., position and orientation) to minimize ghosting. We assess the extent of ghosting using a measure of photo-consistency, which evaluates the similarity in color assigned by the two cameras to the same 3D surface points.

Fig. 8. The scheme shows the reference camera F and the camera to be fine-aligned (M). The images are the actual feed from the physical camera and the rendering with the current extrinsic parameters.

Figure 8 illustrates a common scenario in which two camera frusta overlap. In this context, we will refer to one camera as the 'Fixed' camera (denoted as F), which serves as the reference camera, and the other as the 'Moving' camera (denoted as M), which we aim to align with the fixed camera. We use the notation $I(.)$ to represent the images captured by each respective camera. Both cameras have a partial view of the environment, and their views intersect within a region denoted as R (highlighted in blue in the figure).

Our approach involves texturing the region R by projecting the image $I(F)$ onto it, and subsequently rendering this textured region R from the perspective of camera M. We will denote the set of pixels covered by the projection of R as R_p. In an ideal scenario where the geometry is accurate, and the cameras are perfectly aligned, the projection of the textured scene onto camera M should perfectly match the actual image $I(M)$ within the same portion of the image or screen (assuming also perfectly Lambertian material).

To quantify the disparity between the rendered image and the actual image, we define an error function. This error function serves as a measure of how different the rendering is from the actual image, allowing us to initiate a minimization algorithm. This minimization algorithm adjusts the extrinsic parameters of camera M as variables in order to improve the alignment between the two cameras.

We define our error function using a pixel-to-pixel color difference restricted to R_p, that is, without considering the pixels not included in the rendering. Naturally, such projection changes every time the extrinsic parameters are updated but we are working on the assumption that this is a refinement of an existing camera registration and hence that said change of R_p will be small. Therefore we compute the initial projection and create a mask by dilating it by a certain number of pixels (50 in our experiments). This is a way to restrict the amount of camera movement in a neighborhood of the initial solution. Doing this will tend to avoid local minima of the error function that would be found if R_p could be in every portion of the screen. Please note that bounding the projection can be seen as the output-sensitive alternative to directly apply upper and lower bounds to the parameters (i.e. camera position and rotation).

The exact definition of our error function is given in Eq. 1. N is the total number of pixels, i and j identify the row and column of a pixel position, $Mask(i,j)$ is 1 if the pixel i,j is in the dilated region aforementioned, $colorDist(i,j)$ is the distance between corresponding pixels in the two images and th is a threshold value. Note that the sum is counting how many corresponding pixels in the masked region are closer than a threshold in color space. Hence, the error function (Err) spans the range $[N - N_m, N]$, with N_m representing the count of masked pixels, within a total of N pixels.

We tested several derivative-free minimization algorithms for Non-Linear problems and found the most consistent results with the NEWUOA [32] implementation provided by the C++ library NLOpt [15] The evaluation of $Err(M)$ is carried out by harnessing the graphics hardware. We use a fullscreen quad and provide the image $I(M)$, the result of the rendering from M, and the mask. The fragment shader computes colorDist and *discards* a fragment if the value is below the threshold and the mask value is set 1. On the client side, we use the OpenGL *occlusion query* mechanism to count how many fragments passed the depth test, which in our case means how many where *not* discarded, which turns out to be our Err function. Figure 10 show the same geometry as Fig. 7 after the fine registration step.

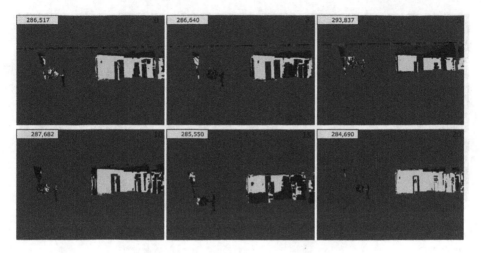

Fig. 9. A sampling of the iterations of the minimization procedure. The function *colorDist* is mapped to the red channel, if the value is below a given threshold (0.2 in this experiment) the pixel is rendered green. (Color figure online)

$$\text{Err(M)} = N - \sum_{\forall i,j} \text{dist}(i,j) \times \text{Mask}(i,j)$$

$$\text{dist}(i,j) = \begin{cases} 1 & \text{if colorDist}(i,j) \le \text{th} \\ 0 & \text{otherwise} \end{cases} \tag{1}$$

Figure 9 shows some steps of the minimization process. The color of pixel (i,j) encodes the value colorDist(i,j) on the red channel (remapped between 0 and 0.5) if it is greater than the threshold, and as green if it is lower than the threshold and if Mask$(i,j) == 1$. Therefore, the amount of green pixels is the result of the summation in Eq. 1.

This procedure should be regarded as a supplementary tool aimed at enhancing registration through point-to-point correspondences, as described in Sect. 4.2. Various scene-dependent parameters influence the final outcome.

One critical factor is the degree of dilation applied to the projection, denoted as R_p. If this value is too large, the minimization process might become trapped in a local minimum. Conversely, if it is too small, there may be insufficient improvement over the initial values.

Another crucial consideration is the precise definition of *ColorDist*. We currently employ the difference in the CIELab color space. However, it's important to note that this implicitly assumes that materials exhibit mostly Lambertian properties, which may not always hold true.

Additionally, the threshold value Th wields significant influence. Setting it too high may result in plateaus in the error function, effectively treating every pixel as a good matching one. Conversely, setting it too low can lead to a discontinuous error function, potentially causing local minima.

Fig. 10. A snapshot of the application with the same geometry as in Fig. 7 after the fine registration step.

5   Real-Time Acquisition and Rendering from LIDAR and RGB Cameras

In our experiments, we tailored the comprehensive system outlined in Sect. 3 to enable real-time acquisition and rendering of multi-sensor data. LIDARs and camera feeds are combined at run-time to offer a free point-of-view rendering. This real-time rendering is achieved through immediate point cloud tessellation and projective mapping, as elaborated in the subsequent explanation.

Tessellation of the Point Clouds. The challenge of defining a 2D surface from a point cloud has a long history with various proposed solutions, as outlined in a comprehensive survey by [2]. The inherent complexities of this problem, such as sparsity and irregular sampling, often require the solver to make assumptions about the nature of the sampled surface. However, in the case of LIDARs, where sampling is partially dense and structured on a grid, it becomes both feasible and reasonable to employ a predefined regular tessellation of the points, simplifying the surface reconstruction process. Note that all of the above does not require any processing on the CPU side, the data arriving from the LIDARs are sent to the GPU as vertices, the tessellation pattern is static and for filtering the triangles we use a geometry shader that discards the unwanted triangles (Fig. 11).

Projecting RGB Images. The final geometry's color is determined through projective texturing [24]. This involves an initial rendering pass in which shadow maps are created for each camera and then utilized in the subsequent rendering pass to ascertain the visibility of each point from different camera perspectives. It is important to note that certain regions in space may be covered by multiple cameras. Consequently, an efficient method is required to merge their often distinct contributions effectively. In our approach, inspired by the work in [5], we blend the contributions of each camera based on the cosine of the angle between the projection direction and the surface normal. Additionally, we enhance image blending in overlapping regions through an image equalization process utilizing histogram matching [31] (Fig. 12).

Fig. 11. Snapshots of the textured geometry with the camera feeds shown at their respective bottom right (from [9]).

Fig. 12. Elongated triangles (in red) usually connect portions of surfaces that are disconnected/different and hence automatically removed. The Left and right images show the same data before and after the removal of triangles (from [9]). (Color figure online)

Remote Rendering. A realistic rendering of the environment is achieved through the tessellated point cloud, followed by projective texturing based on the camera's vantage point. To maintain the quality of the rendered output, rendering data is directly retrieved from the GPU's framebuffer and processed as a stream of JPEG images. The remote rendering process is enabled through a dedicated MJPEG streaming network socket connection, separate from our standard client-server communication. These MJPEG-encoded videos are then transmitted over HTTP protocols, using a highly adaptable, multi-threaded, and computationally efficient streaming framework. This setup allows clients to remotely view real-time rendered content directly in a web browser. In addition to MJPEG streaming, our application provides support for visualizing the rendered content as H.264 streams over the Real-Time Streaming Protocol (RTSP) using the FFMPEG library [40].

6   Conclusion

We introduced an improved version of the system presented in [9] for real-time acquisition and rendering of 3D scenes using low-cost LIDARs and RGB cameras, dubbed NausicaaVR. NausicaaVR supports semi-automatic calibration, on-the-fly tessellation, and remote rendering, and it is built with a client-server architecture.

While our system's results were satisfactory for environmental awareness, challenges remain to achieve immersive real-time rendering. One concern is the precise alignment of data. Even with the improvement proposed in Sect. 4.3 of this paper, spatiotemporal calibration of image and geometry remains sensitive to the specific scene and sensor placements.

One approach worth considering is to project images onto the geometry, even if there's a slight misalignment, and then utilize learning algorithms to minimize or eliminate the ghosting effect. This technique has been employed successfully in related domains like denoising [39] and deblurring [44]. Another obstacle to address is the absence of geometry in areas not captured by LIDAR. These unscanned regions of the scene result in certain parts of the images being projected onto the background as if they were located on the horizon.

One option is to use image segmentation and classification to find parts that are not at the horizon and avoid projecting those pixels if there is no corresponding geometry. This avoids the unpleasant anamorphic effect of misprojection but leaves holes in the rendering. A more intriguing approach is to use image-based techniques to complete the geometry from the existing sampling. In other words, using simple proxy 3D elements for projecting the images. This method would also require precise image segmentation of the images to avoid pixels belonging to the background (e.g., the sky) being projected into such impostors.

References

1. An, P., et al.: Geometric calibration for lidar-camera system fusing 3D–2D and 3D–3D point correspondences. Opt. Express **28**(2), 2122–2141 (2020). https://doi.org/10.1364/OE.381176. https://opg.optica.org/oe/abstract.cfm?URI=oe-28-2-2122
2. Berger, M., et al.: A survey of surface reconstruction from point clouds. In: Computer Graphics Forum, vol. 36, pp. 301–329. Wiley Online Library (2017)
3. Brinkmann, M., Hahn, A.: Testbed architecture for maritime cyber physical systems. In: 2017 IEEE 15th International Conference on Industrial Informatics (INDIN), pp. 923–928 (2017). https://doi.org/10.1109/INDIN.2017.8104895
4. Bu, Z., Sun, C., Wang, P., Dong, H.: Calibration of camera and flash lidar system with a triangular pyramid target. Appl. Sci. **11**(2) (2021). https://doi.org/10.3390/app11020582. https://www.mdpi.com/2076-3417/11/2/582
5. Callieri, M., Cignoni, P., Corsini, M., Scopigno, R.: Masked photo blending: mapping dense photographic dataset on high-resolution 3D models. Comput. Graph. **32**(4), 464–473 (2008). http://vcg.isti.cnr.it/Publications/2008/CCCS08, for the online version: http://dx.doi.org/10.1016/j.cag.2008.05.004
6. Chen, Q., Xie, Y., Guo, S., Bai, J., Shu, Q.: Sensing system of environmental perception technologies for driverless vehicle: a review of state of the art and challenges. Sens. Actuators A **319**, 112566 (2021). https://doi.org/10.1016/j.sna.2021.112566. https://www.sciencedirect.com/science/article/pii/S0924424721000273
7. Corsini, M., Cignoni, P., Scopigno, R.: Efficient and flexible sampling with blue noise properties of triangular meshes. IEEE Trans. Visual Comput. Graphics **18**(6), 914–924 (2012). https://doi.org/10.1109/TVCG.2012.34
8. dSPACE (2021). https://www.dspace.com/en/pub/home/applicationfields/stories/smartkai-parking-assistance-f.cfm

9. Dutta, S., Ganovelli, F., Cignoni, P.: On-the-fly acquisition and rendering with low cost lidar and RGB cameras for marine navigation. In: Grueau, C., Rodrigues, A., Ragia, L. (eds.) Proceedings of the 9th International Conference on Geographical Information Systems Theory, Applications and Management, GISTAM 2023, Prague, Czech Republic, 25–27 April 2023, pp. 176–183. SCITEPRESS (2023). https://doi.org/10.5220/0011855000003473

10. Garrido-Jurado, S., Muñoz-Salinas, R., Madrid-Cuevas, F., Marín-Jiménez, M.: Automatic generation and detection of highly reliable fiducial markers under occlusion. Pattern Recogn. **47**(6), 2280–2292 (2014). https://doi.org/10.1016/j.patcog.2014.01.005. https://www.sciencedirect.com/science/article/pii/S0031320314000235

11. Gong, X., Lin, Y., Liu, J.: 3D LIDAR-camera extrinsic calibration using an arbitrary trihedron. Sensors **13**(2), 1902–1918 (2013). https://www.mdpi.com/1424-8220/13/2/1902

12. Grammatikopoulos, L., Papanagnou, A., Venianakis, A., Kalisperakis, I., Stentoumis, C.: An effective camera-to-lidar spatiotemporal calibration based on a simple calibration target. Sensors **22**(15) (2022). https://www.mdpi.com/1424-8220/22/15/5576

13. Hahn, T., Damerius, R., Rethfeldt, C., Schubert, A.U., Kurowski, M., Jeinsch, T.: Automated maneuvering using model-based control as key to autonomous shipping. at - Automatisierungstechnik **70**(5), 456–468 (2022). https://doi.org/10.1515/auto-2021-0146

14. ImagingSource (2017). https://www.theimagingsource.com

15. Johnson, S.G.: The NLopt nonlinear-optimization package (2007). https://github.com/stevengj/nlopt

16. Kang, J., Doh, N.L.: Automatic targetless camera-LIDAR calibration by aligning edge with gaussian mixture model. J. Field Robot. **37**(1), 158–179 (2020). https://doi.org/10.1002/rob.21893. https://onlinelibrary.wiley.com/doi/abs/10.1002/rob.21893

17. Kim, H., Kim, D., Park, B., Lee, S.M.: Artificial intelligence vision-based monitoring system for ship berthing. IEEE Access **8**, 227014–227023 (2020). https://doi.org/10.1109/ACCESS.2020.3045487

18. Kodaira, A., Zhou, Y., Zang, P., Zhan, W., Tomizuka, M.: SST-Calib: simultaneous spatial-temporal parameter calibration between lidar and camera, pp. 2896–2902. IEEE Press (2022). https://doi.org/10.1109/ITSC55140.2022.9922085

19. Li, Q., Queralta, J.P.n., Gia, T.N., Zou, Z., Westerlund, T.: Multi-sensor fusion for navigation and mapping in autonomous vehicles: accurate localization in urban environments. Unmanned Syst. **08**(03), 229–237 (2020). https://doi.org/10.1142/S2301385020500168

20. Li, X., He, F., Li, S., Zhou, Y., Xia, C., Wang, X.: Accurate and automatic extrinsic calibration for a monocular camera and heterogenous 3D lidars. IEEE Sens. J. **22**(16), 16472–16480 (2022). https://doi.org/10.1109/JSEN.2022.3189041

21. Martelli, M., Virdis, A., Gotta, A., Cassarà, P., Di Summa, M.: An outlook on the future marine traffic management system for autonomous ships. IEEE Access **9**, 157316–157328 (2021). https://doi.org/10.1109/ACCESS.2021.3130741

22. Moghadam, P., Bosse, M., Zlot, R.: Line-based extrinsic calibration of range and image sensors. In: 2013 IEEE International Conference on Robotics and Automation, pp. 3685–3691 (2013). https://doi.org/10.1109/ICRA.2013.6631095

23. Nowicki, M.R.: Spatiotemporal calibration of camera and 3D laser scanner. IEEE Robot. Autom. Lett. **5**, 6451–6458 (2020)

24. NVidia (2001). https://www.nvidia.com/en-us/drivers/Projective-Texture-Mapping/

25. NVIDIA: NVIDIA announces Jetson TX2: Parker comes to NVIDIA's embedded system kit (2017)

26. Paneque, J., Valseca, V., Martínez-de Dios, J.R., Ollero, A.: Autonomous reactive lidar-based mapping for powerline inspection. In: 2022 International Conference on Unmanned Aircraft Systems (ICUAS), pp. 962–971 (2022). https://doi.org/10.1109/ICUAS54217.2022.9836213

27. Park, C., Moghadam, P., Kim, S., Sridharan, S., Fookes, C.: Spatiotemporal camera-lidar calibration: a targetless and structureless approach. IEEE Robot. Autom. Lett. **5**(2), 1556–1563 (2020). https://doi.org/10.1109/LRA.2020.2969164

28. Park, Y., Yun, S., Won, C.S., Cho, K., Um, K., Sim, S.: Calibration between color camera and 3D lidar instruments with a polygonal planar board. Sensors **14**(3), 5333–5353 (2014). https://doi.org/10.3390/s140305333. https://www.mdpi.com/1424-8220/14/3/5333

29. Perera, L., Moreira, L., Santos, F., Ferrari, V., Sutulo, S., Soares, C.G.: A navigation and control platform for real-time manoeuvring of autonomous ship models. IFAC Proc. Vol. **45**(27), 465–470 (2012). https://doi.org/10.3182/20120919-3-IT-2046.00079. https://www.sciencedirect.com/science/article/pii/S1474667016312733, 9th IFAC Conference on Manoeuvring and Control of Marine Craft

30. Peršić, J., Petrović, L., Marković, I., Petrović, I.: Spatiotemporal multisensor calibration via gaussian processes moving target tracking. IEEE Trans. Rob. **37**(5), 1401–1415 (2021). https://doi.org/10.1109/TRO.2021.3061364

31. Pizer, S.M., et al.: Adaptive histogram equalization and its variations. Comput. Vis. Graph. Image Process. **39**(3), 355–368 (1987)

32. Powell, M.J.D.: The NEWUOA software for unconstrained optimization without derivatives. In: Pillo, G.D., Roma, M. (eds.) Large-Scale Nonlinear Optimization, Nonconvex Optimization and Its Applications, vol. 83, pp. 255–297. Springer, Boston (2006). https://doi.org/10.1007/0-387-30065-1_16

33. Rehder, J., Beardsley, P., Siegwart, R., Furgale, P.: Spatio-temporal laser to visual/inertial calibration with applications to hand-held, large scale scanning. In: 2014 IEEE/RSJ International Conference on Intelligent Robots and Systems, pp. 459–465 (2014). https://doi.org/10.1109/IROS.2014.6942599

34. Rüssmeier, N., Hahn, A., Nicklas, D., Zielinski, O.: Ad-hoc situational awareness by optical sensors in a research port maritime environment, approved networking and sensor fusion technologies (2016)

35. Schiaretti, M., Chen, L., Negenborn, R.R.: Survey on autonomous surface vessels: part I - a new detailed definition of autonomy levels. In: Bektaş, T., Coniglio, S., Martinez-Sykora, A., Voß, S. (eds.) ICCL 2017. LNCS, vol. 10572, pp. 219–233. Springer, Cham (2017). https://doi.org/10.1007/978-3-319-68496-3_15

36. Schubert, A.U., Kurowski, M., Gluch, M., Simanski, O Jeinsch, T.: Manoeuvring automation towards autonomous shipping. Zenodo (2018). https://doi.org/10.24868/issn.2631-8741.2018.020

37. Snyder, F.D., Morris, D.D., Haley, P.H., Collins, R.T., Okerholm, A.M.: Autonomous river navigation. In: SPIE Optics East (2004)

38. Thombre, S., et al.: Sensors and AI techniques for situational awareness in autonomous ships: a review. IEEE Trans. Intell. Transp. Syst. **23**(1), 64–83 (2022). https://doi.org/10.1109/TITS.2020.3023957

39. Tian, C., Fei, L., Zheng, W., Xu, Y., Zuo, W., Lin, C.W.: Deep learning on image denoising: an overview. Neural Netw. **131**, 251–275 (2020). https://doi.org/10.1016/j.neunet.2020.07.025. https://linkinghub.elsevier.com/retrieve/pii/S0893608020302665

40. Tomar, S.: Converting video formats with FFMPEG. Linux J. **2006**(146), 10 (2006)

41. Tonnis, M., Lindl, R., Walchshausl, L., Klinker, G.: Visualization of spatial sensor data in the context of automotive environment perception systems. In: 2007 6th IEEE and ACM International Symposium on Mixed and Augmented Reality, pp. 115–124 (2007). https://doi.org/10.1109/ISMAR.2007.4538835

42. Vu, T.D., Aycard, O., Tango, F.: Object perception for intelligent vehicle applications: a multi-sensor fusion approach. In: 2014 IEEE Intelligent Vehicles Symposium Proceedings, pp. 774–780 (2014). https://doi.org/10.1109/IVS.2014.6856588

43. Wright, R.G.: Intelligent autonomous ship navigation using multi-sensor modalities. TransNav Int. J. Marine Navig. Safety Sea Transp. **13**(3), 503–510 (2019). https://doi.org/10.12716/1001.13.03.03

44. Zhang, K., et al.: Deep image deblurring: a survey. Int. J. Comput. Vision **130**(9), 2103–2130 (2022). https://doi.org/10.1007/s11263-022-01633-5. https://link.springer.com/10.1007/s11263-022-01633-5

Approaches for Addressing Spatial Connectivity of Final Harvests Within Forest Harvest Scheduling Algorithms

Pete Bettinger[✉] [iD]

University of Georgia, Athens, GA 30602, USA
pbettinger@warnell.uga.edu

Abstract. Harvest scheduling, or the scheduling of management activities within a forest for a given period of time, is an important aspect of forest planning. Often, harvest scheduling results in a tactical plan that allows forest managers the ability to understand where to go, and what to do, at different points in time. In the development of a harvest schedule, an objective is optimized and constraints are satisfied. As examples, an objective may be to maximize wood produced or revenue obtained over time, or to minimize environmental impact over time. Examples of constraints include restrictions on the flow of wood produced over time, the condition of the standing inventory (uncut forests), the amounts of areas of different management activities, and the location and timing of specific management activities. In many cases, these mathematical problems are formulated either with exact methods (linear or mixed-integer programming) or heuristic methods (simulated annealing, tabu search, genetic algorithms, etc.). This work describes the manner in which the connectivity of final harvests is assessed and controlled in both types of approaches. This work also explores how the control of activities differs between cases (a) when the focus is on controlling the timing of the final harvest of adjacent pairs of forest management units, and (b) when the focus is on controlling how large a collective area might become when multiple adjacent forest management units are scheduled for a final harvest within a given time window.

Keywords: Connectivity · Spatial analysis · Forestry

1 Introduction

Forests provide society numerous benefits, including historically the means by which society builds infrastructure, heats homes and businesses, and cooks food. The benefits derived from forests have been categorized into four common sets of ecosystem services: provisional, regulating, supporting, and cultural [18]. The locations where forest management activities are placed can contribute positively or negatively to the attainment of different ecosystem services, therefore within the scope of forest planning a schedule of future management activities is an important consideration. The management activities

© The Author(s), under exclusive license to Springer Nature Switzerland AG 2024
C. Grueau et al. (Eds.): GISTAM 2023, CCIS 2107, pp. 54–68, 2024.
https://doi.org/10.1007/978-3-031-60277-1_4

that are considered can be influenced by laws and regulations (e.g., [11]), forest certi-
fication guidelines (e.g., [8]) and the interests of the forest landowner. Geography can
also influence the management activities considered, as some management actions may
be better suited to different landscape features, and as some management actions may
be limited based on other nearby management actions (scheduled or implemented).

Forest planning efforts have benefitted greatly from the advancements made in both
computer technologies and geographical information systems (GIS) in the last 40 years.
The mathematical models concerning the management of forested landscapes that can
now be formulated can address very large landscapes and very complex management
actions. The ability to mathematically connect the functional relationships between different ecosystem services (e.g., wood production and wildlife habitat) has also been
facilitated with these advances. One area of harvest scheduling that has attracted a lot
of attention involves the geographic concept of *adjacency*, and concerns over whether
similar management activities are (or will be) placed on the landscape that result in forest
conditions that are too large. For example, the size of final harvest (clearcut) activities
is now regulated in some U.S. states, and therefore two or more final harvests that are in
close proximity (adjacent) may create, ecologically, one rather large area of early suc-
cessional forest condition that violates the regulations. Therefore it has become common
to integrate adjacency relationships into tactical forest planning efforts to devise a plan
that suggests these types of conditions will not be developed.

Aside from adhering to laws and regulations, there are many other reasons why a
forest landowner would want to pursue the development of a tactical forest plan that
includes issues addressing the spatial adjacency of management activities. These can
include concerns about the cumulative effects of forest management and the ability
to develop and maintain suitable wildlife habitat conditions [3, 7] or the size of the
cumulative activities [17]. However, the development of a tactical forest plan is based on
a model of a real world system. The closer the model reflects real world conditions and
issues of concern, the more likely the resulting plan will be implemented successfully.
Unfortunately, some issues, such as the adjacency of management activities, can be
rather difficult to address in a mathematical model. In many cases, the amount of spatial
relationships that need to be recognized can increase exponentially as the size of forest
management units decreases, and as the scope the analysis rules increases. In sum, the
mathematical approaches that could be used to represent important spatial relationships
in a harvest schedule may become burdensome, and tax the abilities of both the planner
and the data development processes that are employed.

In this work, some common approaches for addressing the adjacency of forest management activities, specifically final harvests, within mathematical models employed to
develop a harvest schedule are described. These approaches are described for both exact
and heuristic methods of solving mathematical problems. Further, these approaches are
described for two types of adjacency relationships, one that focuses only on controlling
management activities between pairs of adjacent forest management units, and another
that focuses on a maximum size of management activity, and the adjacent management
units that could be scheduled for final harvest activity at the same time without exceeding
the maximum size.

2 Methods

In this work, the methodological concepts relate to the development of a tactical forest plan, which serves to provide land managers with an idea of where and when forest management activities should be implemented. In the mathematical algorithms associated with contemporary forest management planning, it is possible to control the scheduling of management activities based on their proximity in both space and time. Geographically, the idea that two places are adjacent in space is often based on whether those two places share an edge (line, arc). However, some organizations have defined adjacency based on whether two places share only a single point in geographical space. And, further, if the edges of two places are simply within some distance of each other (yet not physically touching), this can serve as a definition of an adjacent relationship.

In order to set the stage for the work illustrated below, a few definitions are necessary. In forestry, a *management unit* (i.e., stand, polygon) is often defined as a contiguous area of land that will likely be managed as a whole when management activities are implemented. The boundaries of management units are defined using roads, streams, topography, and changes in timber type (age, species, etc.). These features are maintained in a geographic information system (GIS) database, and the adjacency relationships amongst them can be extracted using algorithms that understand the connection or proximity of the edges that form the polygons. Along these lines, *adjacency* refers to the proximity of each management unit to other management units. As noted earlier, two management units might have an adjacency relationship, in spatial terms, when they (a) only share a point (vertex), (b) share an edge, or (c) have edges that are near each other in geographical space. Within quantitative forest harvest scheduling, this information can be of value to prevent the scheduling of two management activities that will conceptually result in a single, larger management activity. The most common example involves final harvests (clearcuts). When two adjacent management units are scheduled for a final harvest during the same time period, the outcome is one larger (the sum of the area of the two management units) final harvest, which may be too large with respect to policies guide forest management. The two types of adjacency relationships commonly recognized in quantitative forest harvest scheduling to control the timing and placement of final harvests are the unit restriction model and the area restriction model [14].

2.1 Unit Restriction Adjacency

In forest management planning, the concept of *unit restriction adjacency* refers to the relationship between only two management units. This relationship notes that one management unit is adjacent to another, and it can be used to control (constrain) the assignment of forest management activities to only one of the two that constitute the pair. For example, if a final harvest were scheduled for one of the two management units, a final harvest would be disallowed for the other during the same period of time. The period of time which is used to disallow a management activity varies from one organization to the next, and perhaps from one set of regulations to another set. Often this period of time is referred to as the *green-up period*, which indicates the amount of time (years) that separate the final harvests of two adjacent management units to allow the new trees in one (the first management unit to be harvested) to grow to a desired height (to allow the management unit to *green up*). In some United States (Oregon and Washington), the green-up period is often assumed to be 4 or 5 years for privately owned forests. On public lands, the green-up period can be much longer. For example, on certain Crown forest lands in Alberta, the green-up period can extend 30 years [9].

Exact Approach. Exact approaches for solving harvest scheduling problems are those that can guarantee that an optimal solution has been located. These include linear, goal, and mixed-integer programming methods among others. For addressing the unit restriction adjacency constraints within a forest harvest scheduling problem, *pairwise constraints* are developed, these types of constraints limit the ability of the optimization process to schedule the same type of management activities to two adjacent management units within a certain period of time. For example, assume there are two adjacent management units, *MU1* and *MU2*. Assume further that for an exact approach decision variables are created to indicate whether management unit 1 or management unit 2 are assigned final harvest actions in period 1 (*MU1P1*, *MU2P1*). With respect to potential actions in subsequent time periods, *Px* will change. For example, *P1* may change to *P2* to represent those activities possible in period 2. Finally, assume that these variables can only be represented by binary integer values in the final solution to the scheduling problem (e.g., *MU1P1* = 1 or *MU1P1* = 0). This would indicate whether a final harvest has been scheduled (1) or not (0) for the management unit during the time period. To prevent the scheduling of final harvests within both management unit 1 and management unit 2 during the same period of time (e.g., time period 1) a pairwise constraint would be developed:

$$MU1P1 + MU2P1 <= 1 \qquad (1)$$

Only one of the two choices is possible when using this type of constraint, limiting actions amongst adjacent neighbours. When there are multiple time periods to consider (when a green-up period is longer than a single time period), additional pairwise constraints are likely necessary.

$$MU1P1 + MU2P1 <= 1 \qquad (2)$$

$$MU1P1 + MU2P2 <= 1 \qquad (3)$$

$$MU1P1 + MU2P3 <= 1 \qquad (4)$$

In the example above, when management unit 1 is scheduled for a final harvest during time period 1 (e.g., *MU1P1* = 1), management unit 2 will not be allowed a final harvest during time periods 1, 2, and 3. These types of equations representing the constraints must be constructed prior to using an exact approach algorithm (e.g., branch and bound, cutting plane, etc.) to solve the harvest scheduling problem. When the definition of adjacency changes, the constraints must be re-constructed. When the green-up assumption changes, the constraints must also be re-constructed.

Heuristic Approach. As a heuristic approach such as simulated annealing or tabu search is being applied to a forest harvest scheduling problem, computer logic is employed to assess resource and policy constraints in real time. For example, if a heuristic attempts to schedule a final harvest for a management unit (say, management unit 1 during time period 1) it will assess potential constraint violations before formally assigning the final harvest period. In other words, when attempting to change $MU1P1$ to 1, rather than 0 (previous value where the harvest was not scheduled for time period 1) all potential wood flow, habitat, adjacency (and other) constraints are assessed using computer logic (If-Then-Else blocks of code and others). To facilitate the assessment of adjacency constraints, an adjacency list is needed. This list indicates the neighbours (in geographic space) of every management unit. The adjacency list is stored in the memory of the computer and accessed when it is needed. An example list below suggests that management unit 1 is adjacent to management units 2, 3, and 4.

management unit, adjacent management unit
```
1,2
1,3
1,4
2,1
3,1
3,4
4,1
4,3
...
```

As you might notice, this list is redundant, which is important when one desires to improve the overall efficiency of the heuristic search process. When the list of adjacency relationships is sorted by management unit number (first value on each line), pointers can be developed to facilitate fast access to only the pertinent information in the list. The pointers for management unit 3, for instance, are 5 (the beginning line number) and 6 (the ending line number). The pointers then serve to direct the heuristic to only the information related to management unit 3 (e.g., the adjacent neighbours of management unit 3 begin on line 5 in the list and end on line 6).

A heuristic process that is designed to assess the final harvest adjacency constraints in a forest management problem would assume first that the time period assigned to a management unit (e.g., management unit 1) is temporarily assigned. Then the status of all adjacent neighbours to the management unit would be assessed to determine whether any one of them is also scheduled for a final harvest during the same time period. If this is the case, a constraint violation is noted, and the temporary assignment of the management unit to the time period is dismissed in subsequent processes of the heuristic (i.e., the final harvest is not allowed.).

```
Constraint violation = 0
For a = Beginning pointer(Management Unit 2) to Ending pointer(Management
unit 2)
    If (Potential harvest period(Management unit 2) = Scheduled harvest
    period(Adjacency list(a))) Then
        Constraint violation = 1
    End If
Next a
```

If the green-up period were assumed to be longer than a single time period, the logic would be enhanced:

```
LowerPeriod = Potential harvest period(Management unit 2) - (Greenup win-
    dow - 1)
UpperPeriod = Potential harvest period(Management unit 2) + (Greenup
    window - 1)
Constraint violation = 0
For a = Beginning pointer(Management Unit 2) to Ending pointer(Manage-
    ment unit 2)
  If (Scheduled harvest period(Adjacency list(a)) >= LowerPeriod AND
  Scheduled harvest period(Adjacency list(a)) <= UpperPeriod) Then
      Constraint violation = 1
  End If
Next a
```

In contrast to the exact approach, when using this logic there would be no need to re-construct the process if the green-up length assumption changes. Here, the *Lower-Period* and the *UpperPeriod* represent bounds (in terms of time periods) on the range of the green-up period. Some additional logic would seem necessary to ensure that the computations of the *LowerPeriod* and *UpperPeriod* are valid for the problem that is being solved (i.e., the lower period is greater than 0, and the upper period is less than or equal to the number of time periods within the time horizon).

2.2   Area Restriction Adjacency

In contrast to unit restriction adjacency, which focuses on only two adjacent management units, an area restriction adjacency issue can involve many management units, depending on the contiguous area of concern. For example, if the contiguous area of final harvest activities is limited to 40 ha, any number of adjacent management units can be scheduled for a final harvest during the same period of time as long as their total area does not exceed 40 ha. This model for controlling the timing and placement of forest management activities on a landscape is more closely aligned with common forestry practices than is the unit restriction model [2]. Further, since the GIS databases that support forest management often contain management units (polygons) of various sizes, when an area restriction for management activities guides the actions of forest managers, some adjacent management units may be combined for simultaneous treatment to improve the efficiency of logging operations (and other processes).

Area restriction adjacency constraints therefore are designed to (a) allow the assignment of similar management activities to two or more adjacent management units during a specific period of time, and (b) disallow this to occur when the total size of the potential block of management units exceeds the maximum area assumed. If the maximum area assumed is relatively small, the number of adjacent management units that might be scheduled for simultaneous activities will also be small. Conversely, when the maximum area assumed is relatively large, the number of adjacent management units that might be scheduled for simultaneous activities may also be large. Assessing the large blocks of similarly treated (in action and in time) management units is the main challenge when using this approach. The area restriction model has been used for controlling the size of final harvests and for building minimum-sized habitat patches [16]. When final harvest sizes are being controlled in a harvest scheduling model, the length of the green-up period complicates the assessment, as the constraint on final harvest size must be viewed from the perspective of each individual management unit. Therefore, the final harvest (clearcut) area may look different from the perspective of each management unit, depending on the time period in which each management unit is scheduled for harvest.

Exact Approach. A number of different methods have been described for controlling the potential assignment of forest harvest activities to multiple management units within a given time frame, while allowing several adjacent management units to be scheduled at the same time as long as the total area does not exceed some maximum area (e.g., [13, 15]. In this work, as in previous work [2], we use the path model [12] since it concisely described an exact approach for addressing area restriction adjacency issues in forest management planning.

Given some maximum area (*MaxArea*) for final harvests (clearcuts) of forests, an exact approach would embark on the development of equations (constraints) that prevent any cluster of adjacent management units from being scheduled for a final harvest at the same time. Conceptually, the equations begin with an adjacent pair of management units. If the total size of these exceeds *MaxArea*, then a simple pairwise constraint (described earlier) suffices to control how large the potential final harvest might become. If the total size of the two management units is less than *MaxArea*, a third adjacent management unit (adjacent to either of the two initial management units) is added to the equation. If the sum of all three management units exceeds *MaxArea*, then a constraint is developed to prevent all three from begin scheduled for harvest during the same time period.

$$MU1P1 + MU2P1 + MU3P1 <= 2 \tag{5}$$

As you can see in this equation, only two of the three management units are allowed to be scheduled for harvest during time period 1, since harvesting all three would exceed the *MaxArea* assumption for final harvests. The process of constructing the constraints continues with all possible combinations of adjacent management units (and their neighbours, and so on), until the *MaxArea* assumption has been exceeded, which then prompts the development of a constraint. Some constraints are redundant.

$$MU3P1 + MU1P1 + MU2P1 <= 2 \tag{6}$$

And some constraints are dominated by others. For example,

$$MU1P1 + MU2P1 <= 1 \tag{7}$$

dominates the previous constraint, since if the result of (7) is true, then the result of (6) will also be true, therefore Eq. 6 is not necessary.

One challenge with this approach for solving a harvest scheduling problem is that all of the constraints must be constructed prior to supplying the problem formulation to a solver (e.g., LINGO 20, CPLEX®, etc.). If the green-up time period assumption is altered (increasing or shortening the time assumed for forests to green up) or if the *MaxArea* assumption is altered, a new set of constraints is needed.

Heuristic Approach. Within a heuristic search process, area restriction adjacency constraints can be assessed in real time. In this case, there is no need to construct the adjacency relationships *a priori*. Each potential final harvest, following the example of this work, would undergo an assessment process before the harvest activity would be formally accepted into a solution. For example, assume that management unit 1 was potentially being scheduled a final harvest during time period 1. A set of logic would be employed to check all adjacent neighbours of management unit 1 for a similar management action during time period 1. If an adjacent management unit is also scheduled for a final harvest during time period 1, the total size of the two management units is determined. If the total size of the two management units does not exceed the *MaxArea* assumption, then management unit 1 can also be scheduled for a final harvest during time period 1. However, most importantly, all adjacent neighbours of management unit 1, as well as all adjacent neighbours of the second management unit that is scheduled for a final harvest during the same time period (and their neighbours, and so on) must be assessed to determine how large the resulting final harvest block might become. The process described below (first offered in [2]) might be used to conduct this analysis.

```
Constraint violation = 0
Block size = Size(Management Unit 1)
Queued(1) = Management Unit 1
Do While Queued (1) > 0
For a = Beginning pointer(Queued(1)) to Ending pointer(Queued(1))
    If (Potential harvest period(Queued(1)) = Scheduled harvest period(Ad-
        jacency list(a))) Then
        Place Adjacency list(a), the adjacent neighbour, in the next empty
            cell of the Queued array.
        Block size = Block size + Size(Adjacency list(a))
        If (Block size > MaxArea) Then
            Constraint violation = 1
            Exit Loop
    End If
End If
Next a
"Seated" Management unit = Queued(1)
Adjust Queued array
Loop
```

This process sets the initial block size as the area of management unit 1 (line 2). Management unit 1 is then "queued" for assessment. As long as there is a management unit in the first cell of the queued array, the process continues. Obviously, at the beginning of this process management unit 1 is in the first cell of the queued array. Pointers to the places in the adjacency list where adjacent neighbours of management unit 1 can easily be found are then used as the beginning and ending points of a For-Next loop (line 5). A question is then asked: if the potential harvest period of management unit 1 is the same as the scheduled harvest period of one of its adjacent neighbours, the adjacent neighbour is then placed into the next empty cell of the queued array. The block size is then increased using the size of the adjacent neighbour, and the constraint is assessed. If the total block size exceeds the *MaxArea* assumption, a constraint violation is noted, and the process terminates. Later, in the heuristic process, this constraint violation is recognized, and management unit 1 is prevented from being scheduled during time period 1. However, if the block size is less than the *MaxArea* assumption, the process checks all other neighbours of management unit 1. When all other neighbours have been checked, and if the block size still has not been exceeded (exiting successfully the For-Next loop) management unit 1 is seated (my term), removed from the queued array, and all other management units in the queued array are shifted one position upward. This suggests that the adjacent neighbours of the adjacent neighbours of management unit 1 will then be assessed. If the entire process does not result in an adjacency violation, scheduling management unit 1 during time period 1 will not result in an area restriction adjacency constraint violation.

The main disadvantage of this heuristic approach is the complex computer logic that is required to efficiently and correctly assess the size of a harvest block. Additional computer logic would also be required when the green-up period is assumed to be longer than one time period of the time horizon. In undergoing this process, it is important to note that the harvest period of the focal management unit (the management unit in position Queued(1)) defines the *LowerPeriod* and *UpperPeriod*.

2.3 Case Study

The case study for this work involves a forested tract of land that is situated in the southern United States, in the southern-most region of Arkansas. The forest (872.7 hectares) is formed as a contiguous tract of land through a collection of 31 management units (Fig. 1) which contain stands of trees of different ages, and contain pine tree species (e.g. *Pinus taeda*, *P. echinata*, etc.) and various deciduous trees (e.g., oaks or *Quercus* spp.) native to the eastern United States.

The tactical forest management plan devised for this property had a 15-year time horizon that consisted of 15, 1-year long time periods. The objective of the tactical plan was to provide a relatively even flow of wood products from the forest, and it was measured in a goal programming sense by minimizing the deviations from a harvest target. The harvest target was defined as an amount less than that suggested using the Meyer amortization volume control method for the forest [4]. For this tract of land, the pre-defined desired sustainable flow of wood products was assumed to be 18,850 tons (2,000 lb per ton) per year. The maximum final harvest size constraint for the area restriction adjacency issue was assumed to be 48.6 hectares (120 acres). Management units that share an edge were assumed to be adjacent. The green-up period was assumed to be 2 years (current year + one additional year). The minimum average harvest age for the trees in each management unit was assumed to be 22 years.

The problem formulations for the exact approaches were developed as mixed integer quadratic programming models which were intended to be solved using LINGO Extended 20.0 [10]. The algorithms for the URM and ARM cases were embedded into a tabu search heuristic that employed search reversion and 2-opt moves [5, 6].

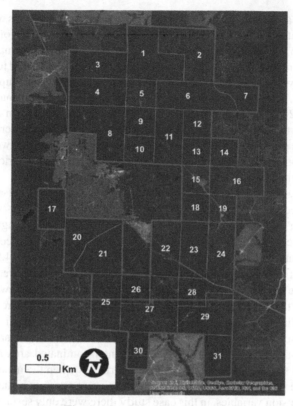

Fig. 1. The case study forest area.

3 Results

For the exact method, 690 non-redundant pairwise adjacency constraints were necessary to address final harvest adjacency restrictions within a single time period when using the unit restriction adjacency model. As the length of the green-up period increased, the number of pairwise constraints increased to 1,978 for two years of green-up (current year + one additional year before and after a scheduled final harvest), 3,174 for three years (current year + two additional years before and after a scheduled final harvest), and 4,278 for four years (current year + three additional years before and after a scheduled final harvest). The increase in necessary adjacency-related constraints was not necessarily linear, since when the green-up period surrounding a proposed harvest (measured in years) extends backwards in time before the initial time period, or extends forward in time beyond the final time period, fewer pairwise adjacency constraints were needed to address these harvest restrictions.

In contrast, when addressing the unit restriction model of adjacency, the heuristic method required no pre-defined adjacency constraints. In this case, the potential adjacency and green-up constraint violations were assessed in real time with each attempted move (shift from one feasible solution to a neighbouring solution) within tabu search. The logic employed to address unit restriction adjacency and green-up constraints within a heuristic can be as minimal as the code that was presented earlier in this work. However, additional computer code is necessary to read, store, and access the list of adjacent management units. To increase the efficiency of this process, pointers (information indicating where the pertinent information begins in the adjacency list) would need to be developed. For the case study forest, an example tactical harvest schedule when employing the unit restriction model, which illustrates the planned harvest period for each management unit, is found in Fig. 2. As you can see, there are two management units in the upper right part of the property that are scheduled for a final harvest during time periods (years) 13 and 15. Since the green-up period is 2 years, this schedule of harvests two years apart is the closest (temporally) possible option when employing the unit restriction adjacency approach, given the assumptions of this harvest scheduling problem.

Again for the exact method, 600 non-redundant, non-dominated adjacency constraints were necessary to address final harvest adjacency restrictions within a single time period when using the area restriction adjacency model. As the length of the green-up period increased, the number of non-redundant, non-dominated adjacency constraints increased substantially to 2,294 constraints for two years of green-up, 4,552 constraints for three years of green-up, and 7,234 constraints for four years of green-up. Like the previous case, the increase was not necessarily linear, and seemed somewhat more exponential in nature than in the unit restriction case. The cause of the increase is based on the number of adjacent management units that can be scheduled for harvest at the same time (relatively speaking) and not exceed the maximum final harvest area assumption. Unlike in previous similar work [2], where one non-dominated area restriction constraint contained six management unit decision variables when the maximum area size was 48.6 ha, and eight non-dominated area restriction constraints contained five management unit decision variables, in this case study there were only seven non-dominated area restriction constraints that contained only three management units.

As suggested earlier, the task of eliminating redundant and dominated constraints from the problem formulation of an exact method can be cumbersome. For example, the area restriction adjacency constraint that allows (at most) only two management units to be scheduled for harvest in a single time period

$$MU1P1 + MU2P1 + MU3P1 <= 2 \qquad (8)$$

is dominated by an equation that relates to only two of the management units

$$MU1P1 + MU2P1 <= 1 \qquad (9)$$

since if the latter (Eq. 9) is true, then the former must also be true. Therefore, the former (Eq. 8) is not necessary as long as the latter is present in the problem formulation.

A unit restriction adjacency model devised for an exact method only requires pairwise adjacency constraints. These are relatively easy to develop (a) when the adjacency relationships are known) and (b) when the green-up is one time period long (the current period of interest). When the green-up period extends beyond the current time period, careful consideration should be applied to the development of pairwise constraints that prevent two or more adjacent management units from being scheduled for harvest within the green-up period. An area restriction adjacency model is more complex in this regard when there are more than two management units within the constraint, and the green-up

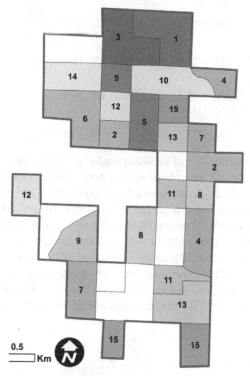

Fig. 2. A forest plan that indicates the time period of final harvests, while accommodating unit restriction adjacency constraints with a green-up length of two time periods.

period is longer than one time period. All possible combinations of potential harvest periods within the guide of the green-up period need to be recognized to prevent the development of a final harvest that in effect is larger than the assumed maximum size. For example, consider three management units (1, 2, and 3). They are each adjacent to each other, and their total size exceeds an assumed maximum final harvest size. If management unit 1 was were to be scheduled in time period 5, and the green-up period was 2 years (years 4, 5, and 6), the following constraints would be necessary to prevent all three management units from being scheduled for harvest in years 4–6:

$$MU1P5 + MU2P4 + MU3P4 <= 2 \qquad (10)$$

$$MU1P5 + MU2P4 + MU3P5 <= 2 \qquad (11)$$

$$MU1P5 + MU2P4 + MU3P6 <= 2 \qquad (12)$$

$$MU1P5 + MU2P5 + MU3P4 <= 2 \qquad (13)$$

$$MU1P5 + MU2P5 + MU3P5 <= 2 \qquad (14)$$

$$MU1P5 + MU2P5 + MU3P6 <= 2 \tag{15}$$

$$MU1P5 + MU2P6 + MU3P4 <= 2 \tag{16}$$

$$MU1P5 + MU2P6 + MU3P5 <= 2 \tag{17}$$

$$MU1P5 + MU2P6 + MU3P6 <= 2 \tag{18}$$

So as it was noted earlier, one of the main challenges for employing an exact method and constraining the timing and placement of forest management activities involves re-constructing the necessary constraint-related equations. One simple change in the assumptions regarding the forest management situation (change in maximum harvest area, change in green-up period assumed) requires re-constructing the constraints.

As with the unit restriction adjacency constraints, the heuristic method has no need for pre-defined area restriction adjacency constraints. An example tactical forest plan representing the scheduled harvest year for each management unit, recognizing area restriction constraints, is found in Fig. 3. As you can see, there are two management units in the upper right part of the property that are scheduled for a final harvest during

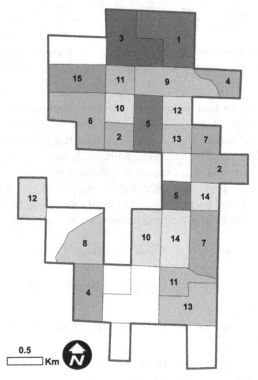

Fig. 3. A forest plan that indicates the time period of final harvests, while accommodating area restriction adjacency constraints with a green-up length of two time periods.

time periods (years) 12 and 13. Since the green-up period is 2 years, this schedule of harvests would not be possible when using the unit restriction adjacency approach. However, since these two management units, in sum, represent an area smaller than the *MaxArea* assumption, they are allowed to be scheduled for a final harvest only one year apart in time.

The potential constraint violations are assessed in real time during an optimization process. As one might imagine however, the computer code and logic required to assess the area restriction adjacency constraints within a heuristic method can be cumbersome. In the example provided earlier in this work, extensive logic would need to be designed to manage the so-called *queued* and *seated* arrays containing management units surrounding a proposed final harvest activity.

4 Conclusions

The approaches for addressing spatial connectivity of forest final harvests within harvest scheduling algorithms have focused here on exact (mixed-integer) and heuristic (e.g., simulated annealing, tabu search, etc.) methods for developing a feasible and efficient tactical harvest schedule. These methods (exact and heuristic) are two lines of inquiry that have captured the attention of researchers over the last 3 decades. While the processes for assessing the unit restriction model of adjacency are relatively straightforward, the exact methods for assessing area restriction final harvest adjacency issues have been well described in the literature (e.g., [12]). And while the processes for assessing unit restriction adjacency within heuristics have been provided in several published papers (e.g., [1, 3, 6]), the logic for assessing area restriction adjacency has only been described theoretically until recently [2].

With exact approaches for assessing final harvest adjacency, the constraints must be developed prior to solving the problem. This is a disadvantage to the approach, and it is further complicated by the fact that the constraints need to be re-constructed if the *MaxArea* or green-up assumptions change. Further, the number of constraints necessary to describe the management problem may grow exponentially depending on the character of the problem (number of management units, size of management units, maximum size assumption, green-up length assumption). With heuristic approaches for assessing final harvest adjacency, the logic employed to correctly assess constraint violations can be cumbersome to develop and time-consuming to assess during the operation of the heuristic. These are disadvantages to the approach. However, constraints do not need to be re-constructed when assumptions regarding the management problem change.

References

1. Akbulut, R., Bettinger, P., Ucar, Z., Obata, S., Boston, K., Siry, J.: Spatial forest plan development using heuristic processes seeded with a relaxed linear programming solution. Forest Sci. **63**(5), 518–528 (2017)

2. Bettinger, P.: Modelling spatial connectivity of forest harvest areas: exact and heuristic approaches. In: Grueau, C., Rodrigues, A., Ragia L. (eds.) Proceedings of the 9th International Conference on Geographical Information Systems Theory, Applications and Management (GISTAM 2023), pp. 136–143. SCITEPRESS – Science and Technology Publications, Lda, Setubal, Portugal (2023)
3. Bettinger, P., Boston, K.: Habitat and commodity production trade-offs in coastal oregon. Socioecon. Plann. Sci. **42**(2), 112–128 (2008)
4. Bettinger, P., Boston, K., Siry, J.P., Grebner, D.L.: Forest Management and Planning, 2nd edn. Academic Press, London (2017)
5. Bettinger, P., Boston, K., Sessions, J.: Intensifying a heuristic forest harvest scheduling search procedure with 2-opt decision choices. Can. J. For. Res. **29**(11), 1784–1792 (1999)
6. Bettinger, P., Demirci, M., Boston, K.: Search reversion within s-metaheuristics: Impacts illustrated with a forest planning problem. Silva Fennica **49**(2), 1232 (2015)
7. Bettinger, P., Sessions, J.: Spatial forest planning: to adopt or not to adopt? J. Forest. **101**(2), 24–29 (2003)
8. Forest Stewardship Council-US: FSC-US Forest Management Standard (V1.1), Complete with: Family forest indicators and guidance and supplementary requirements for lands managed by the USDA Forest Service. Forest Stewardship Council US, Conifer, Colorado (2019)
9. Government of Alberta. C5 forest management plan 2006–2026. Government of Alberta, Edmonton, Alberta (2010)
10. LINDO Systems Inc.: LINGO 20.0. LINDO Systems Inc., Chicago, Illinois (2023)
11. Maine Forest Service: The forestry rules of Maine 2017, A practical guide for foresters, loggers and woodlot owners, 2nd edition. Maine Department of Agriculture, Conservation & Forestry, Maine Forest Service, Augusta, Maine (2017)
12. McDill, M.E., Rebain, S.A., Braze, J.: Harvest scheduling with area-based adjacency constraints. Forest Sci. **48**(4), 631–642 (2002)
13. Meneghin, B.J., Kirby, M.W., Jones, G.J.: An algorithm for writing adjacency constraints efficiently in linear programming models. General Technical Report RM-161, pp. 46–53. U.S. Department of Agriculture, Forest Service, Rocky Mountain Forest and Range Experiment Station, Ft. Collins, Colorado (1988)
14. Murray, A.T.: Spatial restrictions in harvest scheduling. Forest Sci. **45**(1), 45–52 (1999)
15. Murray, A.T., Church, R.L.: Analyzing cliques for imposing adjacency restrictions in forest models. Forest Sci. **42**(2), 166–175 (1996)
16. Sessions, J., Johnson, D., Roos, J., Sharer, B.: The blodgett plan: an active-management approach to developing mature forest habitat. J. Forest. **98**(12), 29–33 (2000)
17. SFI USA: SFI 2022 forest management standard, Section 2. SFI USA, Washington, D.C. (2022)
18. Smart, S., et al.: An integrated assessment of countryside survey data to investigate ecosystem services in Great Britain. CS Technical Report No. 10/07. National Environmental Research Council, Center for Ecology & Hydrology, Wallingford, Oxfordshire, United Kingdom (2010)

An Open-Source Model for Estimating the Need to Expansion in Local Charging Infrastructures

Hana Elattar(✉), Ferdinand von Tüllenburg⑩, Stephan Karas, and Javier Valdes

Institute for Applied Computer Science, Deggendorf Institute of Technology,
Technologie Campus Freyung, Freyung, Germany
{hana.elattar,ferdinand.tuellenburg,javier.valdes}@th-deg.de,
stephan.karas@stud.th-deg.de

Abstract. The growing adoption of electric vehicles (EVs) poses new challenges for the planning and management of charging infrastructures (CIs). This paper proposes a methodology to estimate the sufficiency of EV charging infrastructures in a given area of study (AOS) containing public and private buildings, using open-source data and a case study of Lindau (Bodensee), Germany. The methodology consists of two main steps: first, applying the attractiveness factor concept from travel models to cluster buildings according to their potential EV users; second, classifying charging stations based on their location and occupancy rate. To reach our desired result, we compare the number of charging hours needed by EVs arriving at each building cluster with the number of available charging stations in each station cluster, and identify any gaps or surpluses. The paper demonstrates the feasibility and applicability of the methodology using data from the city Lindau (Bodensee) as an example. The paper also discusses the limitations and assumptions of the methodology, and suggests future directions for developing a machine-learning based tool that could support optimal placement of new charging stations.

Keywords: Electric vehicles (EVs) · Open-data · Charging infrastructure

1 Introduction

In recent years, the distribution of EVs has significantly increased. More and more people switch from combustion vehicles (CVs) replacing them especially with batterydriven electric vehicles (BEVs). Together with the increasing availability of green energy, this development leads to a positive effect for the greenhouse gas balance of our economies. On the other side of the coin, charging infrastructure (CI) is being increasingly requested and utilised. Following the initial spread of publicly available charging stations (CSs) across the countries in order to decrease the hurdles for the shift to more sustainable transportation, now the question arises, at which locations the CI should be strengthened in order to satisfy the needs of the EV users [17].

Several research approaches and studies have been published to evaluate the energy demand and market development of electric vehicles including extrapolations into the nearer future either for particular cities [25] or for whole countries [30]. Other studies answered the question about the current utilisation of CI [11]. In order to estimate arrivals at certain locations it has been proposed to analyse the popularity index (as known, e. g., from Google Maps), showing the occupation of certain locations by time. From these studies, we also know at least in rather general terms how CI needs to be developed in the upcoming years, if this data is compared to scenarios of the future EV market development.

While the given approaches showed their applicability mainly at a larger scale such as whole cities or even countries, they were not applied at smaller areas from districts and areas of a town, nor down to single streets. It is currently unknown and questionable if the given approaches could provide precise information about the CI at such a micro focus. We assume it would require the inclusion of detailed information on the focused area and buildings therein, also including location-specific traffic data. These approaches, that analyse traffic situations at particular locations in order to estimate arrivals, do not take into consideration typical stay times. In addition, for constructing a sound micro-scale CI analysis, the demand of EV drivers should be covered, which is not always considered in the current approaches.

To estimate the degree of disparity between the available CI and the charging demand of particular zones, and finally, to evaluate the extent to which existing infrastructure strengthening is required, the following two questions have been elaborated in our research approach:

First, a suitable methodology for estimating CIs sufficiency in a given area, need to be developed. The methodology in question should be likewise transferable and automated. It should not only consider the traffic situation and the demand coming from the population, but should also cover the reach of charge points which make them attractive to drivers, in particular compared to the typical stay times of the drivers.

Secondly, by preventing the re-invention of the wheel, we aimed to settle on and adapt the already existing approaches. Here, our next question connected; which data is necessary to create a local model at a sufficient precision. This includes also the question of how to automate data gathering, clustering, and evaluation as well as questions about the data precision.

The improved precision- particularly at a small-scale focus- would allow for a more profitable targeted investments into CI, by putting the actual demands of EV drivers into focus. On the one hand it needs to be answered, whether visitors of a certain place find sufficient charging possibilities for their EVs within walking distance. On the other hand, it needs to be considered, whether existing CS are deserted during long periods of time at given locations, which has to do with the time that people typically stay at a given location, state of charge (SOC) of the EV and the users preferences.

Pursuing our objective to develop an approach to estimate the demand for charging in walking distance from particular locations or buildings, we focused on using publicly available data sources. We propose a methodology to determine the use of buildings, which gives an indication of typical stay times and the buildings' opening hours. Additionally, we consider the characteristics of the building such as the size of the building, which gives, together with the building use purpose, an estimation on the maximum number of people that could arrive to the building based on statistical data and building regulations. For the analysis, we limit ourselves to publicly available data to ensure that the approach is transferable to arbitrary regions. The methodology is then based on a re-classification and standardization of OpenStreetMap (OSM) data. Our approach can therefore be well-used as an extension to already existing research directions, which take traffic data and car arrivals at particular locations into their consideration.

As a result, we give an estimation for a given area about the number of people within this area (called the popularity index) during a certain time span. The timely resolution is calculated per hourly rate but can otherwise be freely chosen. Based on this popularity index, we draw conclusions on the possible charging demand.

To test our method, we use it firstly to estimate the hourly charging demand around different types of restaurants within a given city district. We validate our research by comparing our results with other sources and calculate the accuracy of our approach. We applied our approach to analyse restaurants in the city of Lindau (Bodensee), Germany, and obtained for different periods estimations for charging station occupation. Furthermore, we give a short outlook on how the application of AI methods could improve the grade of automation and accuracy of our method, in particular in terms of transferability.

2   Related Work

Our work is based on research that estimates and analyses the loading capacities of EVs and the methods used for it. In our paper [9], we focused on empirical and simulative methodologies.

Empirical methodologies include modelling the energy demand of individual EVs and their drivers, such as van den Akker [16] or Draz and Albayrak [7], and approaches that use available data of charging infrastructure, such as Hecht et al. [11].

Van den Akker proposed a complex model that calculates the energy consumption and charging needs of individual EVs based on more than twenty parameters, such as distance, speed, and slope. However, this model does not consider the reasons for charging that are related to the travel purpose. Draz and Albayrak used a simpler model that only relies on the SOC at arrival time and the battery size of the cars to determine which type of charging station is chosen by the driver. This model also does not directly consider the travel purpose, which might affect the choice of charging type. In our work, we follow a stronger focus on the travel purpose. We also use the model of Hecht et al., who presented a detailed model of occupation times for charging stations at different locations, to estimate the utilization of charging stations near the places under consideration.

Simulative methodologies mainly focused on estimating the energy demand of individual EVs. For example, Schlote et al. [25] combined data about cars' speed with information about tracks' slope in a Markovian model, Koch et al. [18] analysed the energy consumption of different vehicle classes with the traffic simulator SUMO, and Hernández-Moreno et al. [12] created a MATLAB/SIMULINK model for detailed power train simulation of different vehicle classes. A different approach, following the traveling purposes and characteristics of drivers, is followed by Jahn et al., [14] who employed a multi-agent-system (MAS) for describing different daily schedules of people including car driving or other modes of transport.

The approaches of Schlote et al., Koch et al., and Hernández-Moreno et al. follow a deep physical model of individual EVs and their power trains, but consider route characteristics, driver intentions, traveling purposes, and so on only to a limited extent. In comparison, our focus is also on travel purposes, distances, etc., which creates a difference in this aspect. However, it could slightly improve our model if we included particular car types. However, we do not expect a significant impact on the accuracy of our estimation, especially since one of our goals is to provide a forecast on future developments - and the characteristics of future cars would be another source of uncertainty in our assumptions. On the other hand, future developments are part of Jahn et al.'s paper, who considered different scenarios for market penetration of EVs. Their MAS approach would be interesting for later validation of our approach, but this would require some preparation effort and potentially collaboration between our research groups - which we plan to do in a next step.

3   Main Concepts of the Research

It is our goal to develop a methodology to model the traffic energy demand and relate it to the supply provided by existing Charging Stations. The methodology is to be adaptable to different spatial contexts to support with decision-making in planning the local charging infrastructure. Considering that geo-locational differences of different scales (i.e. local, national, or continental) may have implications on the answer to our research question, the key to an easily adaptable methodology relies on the transparency of the included parameters and their effect on the results. This paper discusses therefore two steps to accomplish this purpose:

1. Identification of necessary data
2. Filling the gap in available open and free data
3. The agile calculation methodology

Our research has been developed as part of the CrossChargePoint project, and has been tested on Lindau (Bodensee)- one of the project's areas of study-. In this section we will go through the different types of concepts and data in the area that were found to be available, free, or open for use and that formed the base of our study.

3.1   Breaking Down Travel Models

To calculate the energy needed for traffic, aspects such as the amount of traffic, travel purposes, and variation in the topography, among others, are to be considered [28]. Our paper focuses on the first aspect: The amount of traffic. It considers the availability of free data that can support with such calculation, and abstains from diving deeper into the more in-detail aspects at the current phase. It moves on to using this estimation to highlight the gap between the existing public-charging infrastructure and the demand.

In the field of transport planning, a shift has occurred from estimating the amount of traffic based on statistical prediction on the aggregate-level to focusing on the behaviourally-oriented activity-based approaches. This updated travel modelling approach focuses on studying the reasons behind individual trips, by studying the "travel purpose" and the "measure" (i.e. activity) carried out at the destination. This so-called "activity-based" travel model, takes into account the time intervals of the day as a way to influence the decision to reach different destinations and to conduct various activities. Time in this context is considered as an affecting factor to the travel measure and to the attractiveness of a destination rather than merely for the calculation of the duration of trips [24].

Rising from the activity-based travel modelling logic, we conduct our research by inspecting public buildings as objects of destination. These destinations differ in:

1. Hourly attractiveness factors: the probability of it being chosen as a destination at different times of the day based on the service they provide
2. Building Capacities: Based on regulations assigned to each type of service, a limited sq.m / person is advised.
3. Opening hours
4. Area

These characteristics allow us to divide the day into several time intervals and estimate the amount of people reaching these public buildings during the different intervals and with it the amount of vehicles to be expected to reach them; including - to answer our main research question - electric-vehicles that will require available charging stations upon arrival [9].

3.2 Attractiveness Factors for Public Buildings

Attractiveness factor of destinations signifies the probability a certain destination would be chosen [9]. When investigating the attractiveness factors of different buildings and points of interests (POIs), several sources have been identified. In the work of Klink-erhardt et al. [17] attraction factors of buildings could be used to determine the traffic flow arriving from and to certain points in a city. The approach uses OSM building data as a base where they are clustered into different trip purposes with assigned attractive-ness factors based on the Ver_Bau Programm [3], the FGSV data on building attraction and traffic counts [1], and information shared by popular businesses on the number of visitors.

Inspired by this methodology, our work aims to come up with alternative methods to calculate the attractiveness factors of buildings with different uses and to reach similar results, while avoiding case-specific data sources that cannot be replaced. A main shift in concept has then been made where instead of studying official code data, we went into a more statistical approach of studying past trends and using them for forecast predictions.

3.3 Clustering Charging Stations

Data on charging stations are widely available, with virtually all public or semi-public charging stations offering this data to their users in real-time. However, historical data on their use are not so readily available, in fact, many of the data are not shared by the researchers who have collected them, nor do statistical offices collect these data in a systematic way. Calearo et al. [4] and Firese et al. [10] give us an idea of the difficulty that this represents within a research project since there are no automated means to do this in a systematic way. Hecht et al. [11] have made part of the data public for Germany which have been used intensively for different applications related to the use of CS. Mortimer et al. [21] recently used the data to verify POI attraction models, and their results confirm only that the existence or lack thereof of POIs is not related to the actual installation of CS. Of this list of literature, Hecht et al's work has highly inspired ours. In their work, they provide a calculation of the usage ratio of CSs based on their location (e.g. urban, rural, etc.) during the span of their operation time. With our open-data travel model we can provide a basic estimation of the number of people visiting a certain building during a chosen time interval. The concept of Hecht et al can then overlap our work to categorize nearby CSs based on their study [11].

From OSM and other public sources, we acquire locations and other parameters such as charging power, accessibility, and opening hours of the charging stations currently available in the region under investigation (RUI). However, this data does not contain information on their typical utilisation which can be described mainly by the typical number of charging events per day. As a starting point, we use the classification as proposed by Hecht et al. [11], who classify charging stations according to the location and the nominal charging power. Location classes are "industrial", "urban", "suburban", and "uninhabited", while classes for the charging power are shown in Table 1. The authors provide utilisation profiles for each of these classes by weekday. For our analysis, we use the profiles of "urban"-classed charging stations with 22 kW which is CS class 3 in the provided table. To improve our modelling results we use a correcting factor according to the building classification and the typical stay time.

Table 1. Overview of the five CS charging power classes as defined by [11].

CS class	Charging power
1	$P \leq 4\,\text{kW}$
2	$4\,\text{kW} < P \leq 12\,\text{kW}$
3	$12\,\text{kW} < P \leq 25\,\text{kW}$
4	$25\,\text{kW} < P \leq 100\,\text{kW}$
5	$P > 100\,\text{kW}$

3.4   Data on Electric Vehicles Stock Shares

The estimation of the number of e-vehicles (BEV and PHEV) plays the final role in the prediction of the current energy demand for traffic, and the forecast for future expansion. It is to be derived from general statistical values. For the work on Lindau (Bodensee), we focused on the statistical values for Germany. Official statistics indicate a market share of 2.6% of BEV (1.3%) and PHEV (1.3%) of the total number of vehicles in 2022 [19]. For the development of the market share until 2030 several studies have been conducted, most of them aiming at a total market share of BEV and PHEV between one-fourth [6] and one-third [5]. For 2025, Borscheid [6] assumes a stock share of about 11%.

Thus, for our study, we assume a stock share of BEV and PHEV vehicles of 11% for 2025. For 2030, we assume 30% stock share. The transparency of the methodology and its components, however, reserve the possibility of exchanging this value to that of corresponding new areas of study in the future.

4 Methodology Logic

The main challenge in traffic and CI modelling, aside from identifying and obtaining the required data, is developing of modelling methodologies that can be applied at arbitrary RUIs. This is particularly important as available datasets vary in the degree of detail and between different regions.

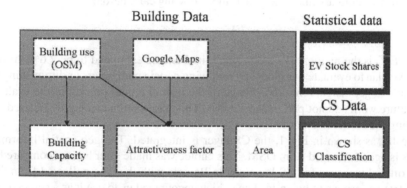

Fig. 1. Methodology Logic.

Our work has started by collecting information on the open and free data that can support in the construction of travel models. Inspired by Klinkhardt et al., as mentioned in the previous section, the path for our research includes the model development based on available OSM data including all available parameters for our selected RUI where we find a outstanding high data accuracy. The resulting model is, in turn, of likewise high quality. Working with OSM data we got to study buildings uses and areas to lay the grounds for calculating the attractiveness factors of public buildings. An important indicator was also found in Google Maps, which provides the user with hourly occupancy rates for popular public spaces that can be studied to identify patterns and creating forecasts. We created our work by combining the available occupancy rates statistics from Google Maps with our OSM data. This overlap allowed us to cluster buildings on OSM and calculate their average hourly occupancy rate of each individual cluster based on the Google Maps statistics. The hourly attractiveness factor used in our study is calculated as the average occupancy rate for said clusters. This attractiveness factor is then multiplied by the maximum capacity in each building to get an estimation of the number of visitors reaching the buildings at different hours. All factors are then added together to calculate the number of visitors reaching each building as per the following equation:

$$V_t = B_c * area * f_a \tag{1}$$

where V_t is the number of visitors for a given hour, B_c is the building capacity - meaning number of sq.m. per person, $area$ is the building floor area, and f_a is the hourly attractiveness factor estimated from the Google Maps statistics. As statistical data on occupational rates are limited whether on GoogleMaps or from official websites, the assigning of attractiveness factor to each cluster helps overcome this gap in data.

The next steps of the methodology are to calculate the number of EVs arriving to each destination and to overlap the CI layer. Assuming all visitors arrive with personal vehicles to the destination- meaning the vehicles count equals the number of visitors (V)-, and taking the EV stock shares mentioned in Sect. 3.4 into consideration, we can use the following equation to estimate the maximum number of EVs (n_{ev}). in this scenario, we could assume based on 1, the following calculation:

$$n_{ev} = EV_s * B_c * area * f_a \tag{2}$$

where EV_s is the national EV stock share, in this case estimated to be 2.6%. In future steps we plan to evaluate our model by removing certain parameters or diminishing their accuracy to get insights into the change of the overall model precision (the evaluation will future work and not part of this article). This information can finally be used when applying the model to other RUIs.

Lastly, as shown in Fig. 1, the CS layer is integrated. The geo-spatial information on CS is again collected from OSM. This choice was made after having compared data from official websites for CS locations in Bavaria with the data collected from OSM. OSMdata has proven to be up-to-date, which encouraged us to use it as a source for this layer of data in order to ensure a harmonized range of data sources. With an important aim of the methodology is to ensure its adaptability, limiting the number of data sources adds a level of robustness. This data is then after subject to classification based on the Hecht et al methodology [11]. The CS are clustered based on their location (i.e. urban, sub-urban, etc.) and assigned an occupancy rate. We know from charging behaviour studies, that an EV stationed in front of a building for a certain duration, will occupy the CS for the same duration; regardless of the time needed to complete a charging profile. It is safed to conclude - based on the mentioned studies- that on average an urban CS is occupied and used 20% of its working time. Time is therefore our point of intersection between the number of EVs, presented in in a destination and the CS demand. Working with the time constraint, we can observe for a certain time interval (Δt), how many hours arriving vehicles would need to be recharged.This will be based on Eq. 2 and multiplying the resulting n_{ev} by the average number of hours to recharge each EV and the hours of charging the nearby CS are fulfilling. The average hours to recharge is estimated to be 2 h to reach an 80% SOC, which is the recommended SOC [2].

5   Methodology Application

In this section we will go step by step into the application of the methodology. As this work has been developed through several phases, we will focus in this article on the new added steps to enhance our methodology, while brushing on previously published phases. In this article we test the methodology by applying it to the area of Lindau (Bodensee) and by limiting the public buildings studied to only include restaurants. Restaurants have been chosen since it is one of the type of public buildings with the most available information online. Google Maps occupancy rates statistics is largely available for restaurants which doesn't limit our study to a narrow set of data, it is also easy to cross check the statistics in the future with the restaurants official websites and social media. We can imagine that by such limitations, the results will not be conclusive but rather lays the grounds for expanding on the logic.

5.1   Working with OpenStreetMap Data

As explained in pevious works [8] & [9], we focus on the work done in Europe and try to clarify what are the current approaches to model traffic or the use of charging stations while relying on open data. From literature, we track the focus on POIs as a main indicator for travel modeling, whether by social sensing [15], based on OSM data [23,27], or Google Maps and Facebook Analytics data [26].

We build up our methodology in accordance with ideas explained in previous literature. The literature involves the work of Pagany et al where the type of POIs are used to calculate the dwelling times of visitors [23], and that of Hummler et al. where the distance between POIs and CSs is used to calculate the attractiveness of said stations [13]. Both uses serve in the development of CI and traffic planning. OSM is proven to be one of the largest sources of open-source data and the most-known voluntary map

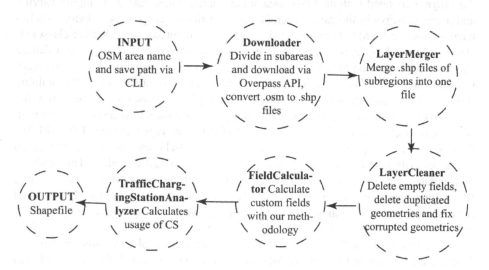

Fig. 2. Steps sequence of the data processing pipeline, extract from Elattar et al. [8].

worldwide [9]. Our motivation to use OSM as a base for our work is thanks to its worldwide availability and its flexibility in regard to both adapting the data and validating it. A more important benefit is the unlimited possibility to extract data from OSM, which feeds directly into our logic of having an worldwide adaptable model, which in turn increases in accuracy and homogeneity the less variety of sources are involved . With the focus of adaptability, it was important to download all existing buildings and POIs in the area of the city of Lindau at Lake Constance in Bavaria, Germany. From the base data We consider all polygons and POIs as the travel destinations for our model [8,9].

Framework for OSM Data Classification. Taking the characteristics of the city of Lindau (Bodensee) as inputs, we started the process of applying our logic and visualizing the results on the map using Geographical Information System (GIS) software. We followed the logic sequence as shown in Fig. 2 to create an automated data pipeline. This pipeline extracts all buildings and POIs falling inside certain administrative boundaries then proceeds to clean-up the data and calculate all needed fields for our travel model. Founded on PyQGIS, an Application Programming Interface (API) for the opensource Geographic Information System (GIS) application QGIS[1], we were able to build a modular standalone data processing pipeline. The pipeline includes multiple independent modules representing each step of data processing, as shown in Fig. 2 that can be executed as needed. The workflow includes the downloading, aggregation and classification of the OSM base data. The only dependency is a valid, platform independent, QGIS (in our case QGIS LTR 3.22.x). The detailed explanation of the the pipeline, including codes extracts, can be found in the Elattar et al. [9].

The pipeline merges between algorithms that are built in QGIS and explicitly written codes. It works on deleting duplicates, merging all layers, cleaning out empty attributes, and exports the output in a shapefile format.

The most critical module of the pipeline is the `FieldCalculator`. In this phase, the `tags` associated with the OSM data are extracted. These `tags` are highly varying and are not always in the same order. Because of this heterogeneity, previous studies have focused on OSM data that have already been structured around feature classes (f-classes). In machine learning, a feature is a specific property of an object and feature classes are a collection of features describing sets of similar objects. This in our case, translates into an"f-class" that represents the main amenity or service of the building (other than residential). In the case of Valdes et al. [27], f-classes are derived from the Grofabrik database and aggregated, in this study we use a similar methodology, but with defining the f-classes ourselves based on the OSM feature tags from the OSM API. We do this in order to apprehend details that pre-defined f-classes from other sources do not necessarily take into account and that are specific to traffic models. This leads us to generate a tree of f-classes that are compatible with the needs of traffic modelling, by having f-classes represent possible destinations, and which could again be modified if the spatial context demands it (i.e. adding new fclasses or removing country-specific ones).

The purpose of the `FieldCalculator`-module is to calculate missing fields in OSM, needed to apply the methodology logic explained in Sect. 3. For that, we begin

---

[1] https://www.qgis.org.

with creating new attribute fields ("fclass", "build_cap", and "area") on the polygon layer by using the "layer_provider.addAttributes()" function. After that the module iterates over each polygon feature. We begin be determining the "fclass" by comparing the"amenity", "leisure", "office", "tourism", "shop" and "building" fields. Going forward the polygon area in square meters is calculated and saved in the "area" field by using the "QGSDistanceArea().measureArea()" function. After that the "build_cap" field representing the building capacity of sqm/ person * area. This field is assigned by cross-referencing the official architectural recommended standards published by sources of official codes and architectural standards [22] and multiplying by the building area. An extract of that matrix looks as such:

```
FCLASS_TRAFFIC_MATRIX = {
'restaurant': {
    'area': 'Restaurant',
    'buil\_cap': '111.83',
    'area': '159.76'
}, ... }
```

The module finishes by selecting all features in the layer and saving them to the user-defined output directory as a copy with the "native:saveselectedfeatures" algorithm. The output is saved in both a shp and json file formats. The buildings classification then resembles the map shown in Fig. 3, with residential buildings marked as unclassified. Residential buildings have been subtracted for this phase of the research

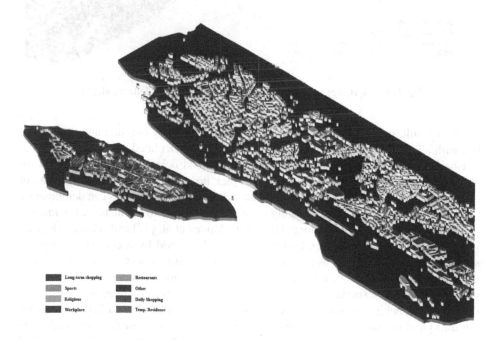

Fig. 3. Classified OSM Buildings, extract from Elattar et al. [8].

since they require a more detailed study as they represent start points of trips as much as destinations, have different demographics, and require investigating the presence of private CS.

The "TrafficChargingStationAnalyzer"-module proceeds then to iterate over OSM mapped charging stations (downloaded again by the "Downloader"-Module, but querying this time for "charging_stations"), calculates a 400-meter buffer (native "geometry().buffer()" function) around it as shown in Fig 4.

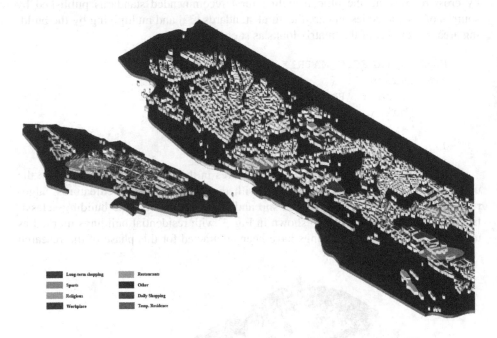

Fig. 4. 400-m Buffer around CS in Lindau, extract from Elattar et al. [8].

As a result, there are two layers, one shapefile with every building and one shapefile with all charging stations and their corresponding calculated values. The pipeline finishes by validating if the output file exists and then deleting all temporal files. In case something goes wrong, the pipeline can pick up at a user controllable step so not everything needs to be run again. Having automated these calculations can demonstrate the variation in which existing charging stations will answer to the increased demand.

Some problems already highlighted in both Valdes et al. [27] and Klinkhardt et al. [17]'s works, lie in how a given POI is represented in OSM by users. For example, a supermarket can be entered as a point or a polygon. If it is a point, it can stand alone or in combination with other POIs on or outside the same building. In the case of a polygon, it can be a single polygon or be composed of several polygons representing the same POI, but it may or may not be labelled as a single POI. The API combined with our data pipeline allows us the freedom of classifying the data based on our needs.This also gives us the freedom of checking and re-working the tags if the spatial context demands it.

5.2 Working with Google Maps

Despite our focus of predominantly utilizing open-source data, our data sources include Google's Places API. Although Google's API doesn't fall under the category of open-source data, it does contain a large amount of free available data which provide extensive and relevant information that complements that of OSM. Google's Places API offers a vast amount of relevant and detailed data that enriches our dataset. This includes valuable insights such as user reviews, popular times, ratings, and other relevant information about establishments.

As explained in the previous section, we developed our own data aggregation pipeline, appropriately harnessing the data from these sources to our liking into a .shp format dataset. The output from the data extracted from OSM and explained in Sect. 5.1 is in both .shp and .json file formats. This JSON file serves as the foundation which our GoogleMaps process builds data upon. To retrieve additional data off Google, the Google Places API requires a PlaceID, a unique identifier assigned to each establishment by Google. Google's Python library is leveraged with its reverse_geocod(latlng) function which acquires the PlaceID for each restaurant using its coordinates that are extracted from the OSM data in a tuple as a parameter. With Google's"Popular Times" data being essential for the model and not being readily available by Google's API, an external open-source API built upon Google's is utilized for the task.

6 Estimating the Attractiveness Factor

For our methodology to remain open and adaptable, a shift from direct attractiveness factors to a calculation of visitor rate- and with which number of vehicles- was decided. Building on the concept of attractiveness factor, we consider in this paper the Google analytical statistics attached to public spaces and POIs.

In our pursuit of data analysis, we deploy a clustering methodology rooted in the classification of restaurants based on the count of meals they serve, as shown in Fig. 5. This categorization strategy empowers us to unveil groups of restaurants with aligned operational characteristics. This step underpins our comprehension of occupancy dynamics within distinct dining environments and facilitates the tailored design of predictive models for enhanced accuracy.

To facilitate the clustering of the restaurants, we employ a predefined dictionary named MEAL_TYPES, encapsulating the impact of varied meal types on the restaurant's operational intensity. For instance:

```
MEAL_TYPES = {
"serves_breakfast": 1,
"serves_dinner": 4,
"serves_lunch": 2
}
```

This deliberate association of meal types with numerical weights imparts nuance to our portrayal of a restaurant's activity levels.

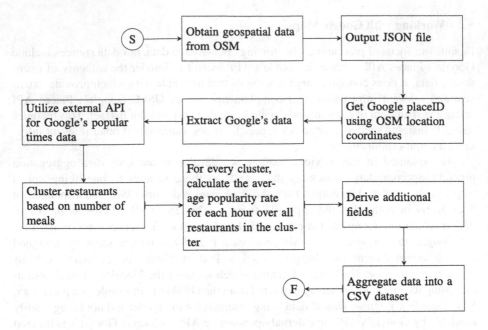

Fig. 5. Framework for data aggregation and clustering.

The `calculate_average_popularity_rates` function computes the mean popularity rate for each hour across restaurants in the clusters grouped by the number of meals served (*num_meals*). It iterates through each hour in each cluster's popularity rates, excluding restaurants with missing or invalid data. The algorithm accumulates popularity rates for each hour, dividing by the total number of valid restaurants to determine the average. This process yields a dictionary which maps each *num_meals* to an array of average popularity rates for each hour. The function's methodology ensures robust insights into temporal consumption patterns, aiding predictive modelling endeavours.

```
# Looping through each cluster of restaurants grouped by
num_meals:

for num_meals, cluster_data in restaurants.items():
    popularity_rates = cluster_data["popularity_rates"]

# Initializing a list to store the average popularity rates:
for each hour
    avg_hourly_rates = [0.0] * 120  # 120 hours (5 weekdays
    * 24 hours)

# Calculating the average popularity rate for each hour:
    for hour in range(120):
        avg_hourly_rates[hour] /= num_restaurants
```

The structure of the clustered restaurants dictionary which calculates the average popularity rates takes as input is as follows:

```
restaurants = {
1: {
    "num_meals": 1,
    "popularity_rates": [
        [popular_times for restaurant 1],
        [popular_times for restaurant 2],
        ...
    ]
},
2: {
    "num_meals": 2,
    "popularity_rates": [
        [popular_times for restaurant 1],
        [popular_times for restaurant 2],
        ...
    ]
},
...
}
```

From the research of Sparks et al. [26], we get an understanding of how temporal signatures for different POIs differ based on the spatial context [26]. These patterns are affected by the cultures inhabiting the city, which religion is dominating, and the different times of the year (i.e. different seasons, periods of cultural or religious significance - as is the case for the Christmas season - etc.). In our current research, we focus merely on testing our methodology in the span of a normal time period while focusing on weekdays which are usually more stable and predictable than weekends. We have collected the occupational rate statistics available on GoogleMaps for all of the restaurants, then proceeded to cluster them based on $\Sigma number of meals$. In Fig 6 we can see that 3 different clusters of restaurants have been formed, including an unclassified range of restaurants. We then proceeded to collect the hourly occupational rate for all the restaurants and calculate the average hourly rate for each cluster.

With the discrepancy between the data available on the number of meals and that of the hourly occupational rate, identifying the hourly attractiveness factor per cluster allows us to overcome this gap.

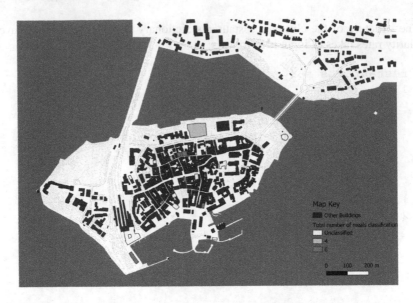

Fig. 6. Extract of the map of Lindau, showing different restaurants clusters.

7 Results

We applied all the previous steps and moved on to zoom in on our results. Focusing on one charging station and the restaurants within a walking distance of 400m from it, we were able to apply Eq. 2 on the data we have. The result is an hourly estimation of the number of EVs in the surrounding restaurants that is then converted to a number of hours of charge (HOC) representing the demand. The same number is calculated for the CS in the area which represents the number of HOC that the CS covers. As shown in the graph in Fig. 7, we can track which hours of the days the demand of EVs exceeds the coverage of nearby CSs. We can conclude that during the first hours of the day and until 8 in the morning, CSs can fulfill almost 100% of the energy demand from traffic, while as the rest the day and until midnight, the fragment of fulfillment of CSs becomes very narrow. This indicates that visitors to the restaurants cannot reach their destinations while depending on the public CI.

These results convey a further meaning. The lack of dependency on public CI leads to the discouragement in switching to BEV, for instance for residents of apartment buildings that fail to find the space for a privately owned CS. It can also showcase how the percentage of fulfillment of CSs would look like in the next years. Based on the stock shares concluded for EVs (2,6% for 2022, 11% for 2025 and 30% for 2030), we can extrapolate the same graph and provide a forecast for the future need of expansion CI.

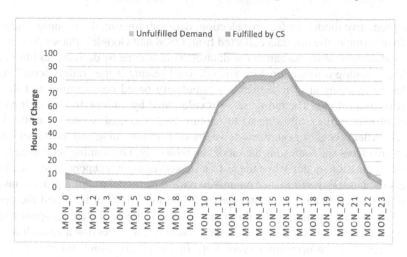

Fig. 7. Chart representing the total hours of demand for EVs arriving to restaurants in relation to the demand covered by the nearby CS.

8 Future Work

As presented in our paper, our methodology allows for the estimation of the number of e-vehicles reaching different public destinations that can be applied to different contexts and hence allow for the enhancement of local charging infrastructures. In this part we delve into the development of a machine learning model for hourly occupancy prediction of any public place across the globe. A subsequent step we're taking is developing a machine learning model for hourly occupancy prediction in restaurants. By starting with restaurants, we can gather data, refine the model, and understand the factors that influence occupancy. Once perfected, we will then adapt the model further to more public spaces. This involves a prediction of the rate or the number of persons present at a particular restaurant and time.

The work is planned to be expanded to involve more public buildings, but also to fill the gap in the missing data. We plan to rely on MachineLearning to fill in all necessary information that will enhance our results, such as filling in the missing statistics from GoogleMaps, whether for other types of buildings or for non-classified buildings. In addition to the raw data collected from OSM and Google's Places API, we also derive additional features to enrich our dataset. One such derived feature is the "rating_score", which provides an assessment of a restaurant's popularity based on its rating and the total number of user ratings. The rating_score is calculated by multiplying the rating by the number of user ratings, allowing us to capture both the quality and quantity of user feedback.

8.1 Machine Learning Logic

A linear regression approach was chosen for its simplicity and ability to capture linear relationships between data fields and the target variable. The key steps involved in building the predictive model are feature selection, data splitting, model training, and evaluation. In addition to the raw data collected from OSM and Google's Places API, we also derive additional features to enrich our dataset. This is done by deriving additional features from existing information. One such derived feature is the "rating_score", which provides an assessment of a restaurant's popularity based on its rating and the total number of user ratings. The rating_score is calculated by multiplying the rating by the number of user ratings, allowing us to capture both the quality and quantity of user feedback. After processing our dataset, we divide it into training and testing subsets for training the model and for testing the model on relatively. The training set is used to train the linear regression model, while the testing set serves as an independent evaluation set to assess the model's performance on unseen data. The model training process involves estimating the coefficients (weights) for each feature. The goal is to find the optimal set of weights that minimises the difference between the predicted occupancy values and the actual observed values. Overall, the chosen linear regression approach provides a solid foundation for occupancy prediction. Its simplicity allows for easier interpretation of results, enabling stakeholders to understand the impact of different features on occupancy levels. By carefully selecting relevant features, splitting the data, and employing appropriate training techniques, we can develop a robust predictive model that captures the underlying dynamics of occupancy and enhances decision-making in various domains.

9   Validation

At the current state of our work a complete validation of our approach is not feasible due to missing real-world data on EV charging. Although there are data sources for charging stations showing their utilisation and number of charging processes, background information on charging activities, such as motivation for charging, reasons of a trip, etc. is not available. In our future work, we plan to empirically study these necessary backgrounds but at the moment, we suffer additionally from the still rather small market penetration of EVs. At the moment, this makes it generally hard to draw universally valid conclusions.

As we keep to provide a true validation of results by comparing the results of our approach with the real-world truth or the results of comparable approaches as future work, we focus more on the conceptual or technical validation of our approach. One approach is the validation by comparing our results with Google's popularity index, the other validation approach uses traffic counting information combined with a EV driving simulation.

9.1   Validation by Popularity Index

The basic idea is to validate our clustering methodology as it has been described in Sect. 6 by applying the trained system to another area that has not been analysed before and compare the results with comparable data coming from other sources. For instance, after we applied our method to a region and computed the utilisation of a restaurant for a given time span, we could compare that value with the value coming from Google's popularity index. For the validation it is necessary, however, to select buildings which fits best to the learned cluster properties. In case of deviations between our results and the reference values, we have the possibility to discuss reasons based on the deviations between the values. In this way the confidence and reliability of our method can be strenghtend.

Figure 8 depicts the validation approach using Google's popularity index. In the first step we apply the previously learned clustering method to new AOS. For validation the buildings with best fits in each cluster are selected for validation. Besides having the best fitting score, of course the reference value (in this case the Google popularity index) must be available. In the next step, the calculated utilisation estimation is extracted. Then, in case of Googles popularity index, the time span considered needs to be adapted for both values to describe the same period, before the values can be directly compared, and potential differences could be discussed.

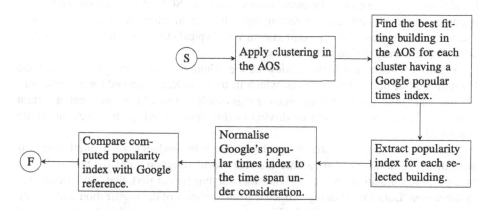

Fig. 8. Approach for validation of the popularity index.

We applied this validation approach to a selection of three restaurants in the city of Passau, in Bavaria. The choice of study comes from it adhering to the same social and economical aspects as our main AOS Lindau (Bodensee); both cities are located in Bavaria, and sharing aspects such as high tourists rates. The restaurants selected in Passau were the ones best fitting to the cluster of restaurants serving lunch and dinner but no breakfast. The accuracy of our prediction was compared on an hourly basis. This means that for every hour of the day, we compared how accurate our prediction is compared to the data stemming from the Google popularity index. The accuracy ranges between 0 % (mainly at the boundaries of the opening hours) and over 90 % especially at times, which hold a strong occupation of the restaurants (during typical lunch and dinner times). Considered the whole day, a total accuracy of about 65 % has been achieved with the developed approach. This numbers unveil that there is still room for improvement of our approach. Furthermore it unveils that probably the number of training data is still low, which is indicated by the fact that the accuracy is significantly higher during time periods when restaurants for lunch and dinner are typically open, while it drops in times at the margins of typical opening hours.

9.2 Validation by Simulation

The validation by simulation approach aims at validating the estimated utilisation of charging stations in the AOS by comparing our mainly data-analytical approach with estimations coming from a simulation. Even if it is not in every case possible to directly compare the actual result values quantitatively, a qualitative comparison of the results is still possible. This includes, for instance, to discuss reasons of large differences of the results of the tow approaches in order to develop confidence in the approach and create awareness of different influence factors for estimation of charging station utilisation.

For the simulative validation approach, we use traffic data of the AOS in form of source and destination traffic. This data may come from public available results of official traffic counting campaigns conducted by public authorities, as well as from publicly published voluntary traffic counting activities. Having this data, we already have an indication regarding the number of cars coming to the AOS at a given time span. In addition to this, we can take assumptions about the SOC of the cars coming to the location, and thus, their need for recharging. This would allow us, in turn, to estimate average charging times and, in combination with typical stay times, also the utilisation of a given charging station at a given location.

Figure 9 provides a schematic view of the simulation used for validation. At the beginning some boundary conditions which fit to the AOS are defined for a single simulation run. This contains of a specific car class such as a small passenger car, a certain driving style such as energy-aware driving or time-aware driving, third a certain route is defined.

In order to obtain a realistic view, it is necessary to conduct several simulation runs with modified parameters to capture the real-world situation valid for the AOS. For instance, the simulation runs should consider the typical car park that can be expected in the region. Data can be easily extracted from statistics of car registration authorities, which are usually publicly available. Furthermore, a realistic set of driving styles should be covered, which can also be obtained from statistics. Third, the source and destination

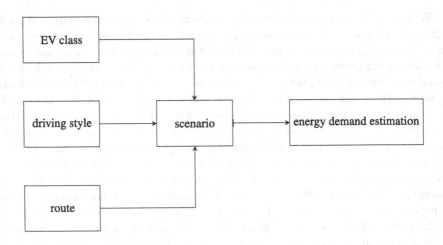

Fig. 9. Schematic of the simulative approach.

traffic information is used to create the set of most typical routes drivers in the region take at the AOS. The routes not only cover the distance of driving but also considers typical driving speeds and topological data of the routes. The scenarios are the encoded as digestible input for a simulation tool, which is capable of calculating the energy demand of a specific ride.

10 Conclusion

Based on previous literature, such as that of Wirges et al., we know that some constraints exist when aiming to expand the regional CI [29]. Over-saturation of local areas with CSs can lead to the business becoming more costly than profitable, meaning that the losses from unused CSs can exceed by far their use profit which would discourage investors from entering such business. This economic factor among others, like grids capacities, traffic regulations prohibiting driving in some areas, and the existence of a large network of private CSs, highly affect the decision-making of CI planning.

Considerably, not all factors are considered in this study, neither is it the intention to bring all factors into the study. The aim is mainly to come in terms with the disparities between the existing CI and the plan of EU countries to phase out internal combustion engine vehicles between the years 2030 and 2040 [20]. For the estimation of the needed expansion in local CI, relying on commercial data provides the highest accuracy, and reduces the cost factor by eliminating unnecessary developments or new installations. However, such accurate results are not indispensable for our specific analysis on disparity. As researchers, we can rely on open-data to overcome the scarceness and cost of commercial data and reach our answer. Looking at the results from the previous section, it is easy to spot at this level of the study that the public CI does not match up to the needs of the public. The graph still needs to be enhanced by eliminating assumptions and calculating the number of EVs for all buildings. Still the graph provides a good indication of the hours of the day when a larger CI would be needed. This information is key to the decision on how large should the expansion actually be, to avoid an accumulation of dormant CSs of more than 50% of the working hours of said CSs.

Adding to this, it is important to highlight the use of Machine Learning in this process. Although our study has only laid the grounds for what the use of Machine Learning in the next steps, it is important to note the correlation between enhancing our results and automating the process. It is not only a matter of speed but more importantly it is needed for data enhancement. Using synthetic and predicted data can enhance the accuracy of our model. Moreover, for other areas of investigations (e.g. rural areas), using such synthetic data becomes a need to reach results that can otherwise be put on a halt.

Lastly, however adaptable and transparent the model is, it is necessary to take a precise look at the study of area, meaning by understanding the different factors to consider and what could potentially be overlooked; which incidentally was the aim in making the model as transparent as possible. This in-depth look would be especially necessary in interpreting the results.

References

1. Hinweise zur Schätzung des Verkehrsaufkommens von Gebietstypen (2006)
2. Abdi, H., Mohammadi-ivatloo, B., Javadi, S., Khodaei, A.R., Dehnavi, E.: Chapter 7 - energy storage systems. In: Gharehpetian, G., Mousavi Agah, S.M. (eds.) Distributed Generation Systems, Butterworth-Heinemann, pp. 333–368 (2017). https://doi.org/10.1016/B978-0-12-804208-3.00007-8, https://www.sciencedirect.com/science/article/pii/B9780128042083000078
3. Bosserhoff, D.: Programm VER_bau: Abschätzung des verkehrsaufkommens durch vorhaben der bauleitplanung mit excel-tabellen am PC (2003). https://www.dietmar-bosserhoff.de/index.html
4. Calearo, L., Marinelli, M., Ziras, C.: A review of data sources for electric vehicle integration studies. Renew. Sustain. Energy Rev. **151**, 111518 (2021)
5. Center of automotive management: electromoility report 2022 (2022)
6. Detlef Borscheid, Kraftfahrt-Bundesamt: Prognose: Mehr als elf Millionen Elektroautos und Plug-Ins bis 2030. Autohaus (2020)
7. Draz, M., Albayrak, S.: A power demand estimator for electric vehicle charging infrastructure. In: 2019 IEEE Milan PowerTec, pp. 1–6. IEEE (2019). https://doi.org/10.1109/PTC.2019.8810659
8. Elattar, H.: Open-data methodology for optimizing the allocations of Charging Stations
9. Elattar, H., Von Tüllenburg, F., Wöllmann, S., Valdes, J.: Evaluating the fulfilment rate of charging demand for electric vehicles using open-source data. In: Proceedings of the 9th International Conference on Geographical Information Systems Theory, Applications and Management. SCITEPRESS - Science and Technology Publications, Prague, Czech Republic, pp. 159–166 (2023). https://doi.org/10.5220/0011849400003473, https://www.scitepress.org/DigitalLibrary/Link.aspx?doi=10.5220/0011849400003473
10. Friese, P.A., Michalk, W., Fischer, M., Hardt, C., Bogenberger, K.: Charging point usage in Germany-automated retrieval, analysis, and usage types explained. Sustainability **13**(23), 13046 (2021)
11. Hecht, C., Das, S., Bussar, C., Sauer, D.U.: Representative, empirical, real-world charging station usage characteristics and data in Germany. ETransportation, **6**, 100079(2020). https://doi.org/10.1016/j.etran.2020.100079
12. Hernández-Moreno, A., et al.: Transient traffic energy-use analysis employing video-tracking and microscopic modeling techniques: a case study using electric and combustion engine vehicles. Energy Sci. Eng. **10**(7), 2022–2034 (2022). https://doi.org/10.1002/ese3.1148
13. Hummler, P., Naumzik, C., Feuerriegel, S.: Web mining to inform locations of charging stations for electric vehicles. In: Companion Proceedings of the Web Conference 2022, pp. 166–170 (2022). https://doi.org/10.1145/3487553.3524264, http://arxiv.org/abs/2203.07081, arXiv:2203.07081 [cs]
14. Jahn, R.M., Syré, A., Grahle, A., Schlenther, T., Göhlich, D.: Methodology for determining charging strategies for urban private vehicles based on traffic simulation results. Procedia Comput. Sci. **170**, 751–756 (2020). https://doi.org/10.1016/j.procs.2020.03.160
15. Janowicz, K., Gao, S., McKenzie, G., Hu, Y., Bhaduri, B.: GeoAI: spatially explicit artificial intelligence techniques for geographic knowledge discovery and beyond. Int. J. Geogr. Inf. Sci. **34**(4), 625–636 (2020)
16. Akker, J.M. van den.: E-Vehicles: Interaction of Smart Charging and DSO Strategies. Utrecht University (2020)
17. Klinkhardt, C., et al.: Using OpenStreetMap as a data source for attractiveness in travel demand models. Transp. Res. Rec. **2675**(8), 294–303 (2021). https://doi.org/10.1177/0361198121997415

18. Koch, L., et al.: Accurate physics-based modeling of electric vehicle energy consumption in the SUMO traffic microsimulator. In: 2021 IEEE International Intelligen Transportation Sys tems Conference ITSC, pp. 1650–1657. IEEE (2021). https://doi.org/10.1109/ITSC48978. 2021.9564463
19. Kraftfahrt-Bundesamt: Der fahrzeugbestand am 1. januar 2022 (2022)
20. Mock, P.: European union co2 standards for new passenger cars and vans (2021)
21. Mortimer, B.J., Hecht, C., Goldbeck, R., Sauer, D.U., De Doncker, R.W.: Electric vehicle public charging infrastructure planning using real-world charging data. World Electr. Veh. J. 13(6), 94 (2022)
22. Neufert, E., Neufert, P., Kister, J.: Architects' data. Wiley-Blackwell, Chichester, West Sussex, UK ; Ames, Iowa, 4th ed edn. (2012), oCLC: ocn775329524
23. Pagany, R., Marquardt, A., Zink, R.: Electric charging demand location model-a user- and destination-based locating approach for electric vehicle charging stations. Sustainability 11(8), 2301 (2019)
24. Pinjari, A.R., Bhat, C.R.: CHAPTER 17. Activity-based Travel Demand Analysis
25. Schlote, A., Crisostomi, E., Kirkland, S., Shorten, R.: Traffic modelling framework for electric vehicles. Int. J. Control 85(7), 880–897 (2021). https://doi.org/10.1080/00207179.2012. 668716
26. Sparks, K., Thakur, G., Pasarkar, A., Urban, M.: A global analysis of cities' geosocial temporal signatures for points of interest hours of operation. Int. J. Geogr. Inf. Sci. 34(4), 759–776 (2020)
27. Valdes, J., Wuth, J., Zink, R., Schröck, S., Schmidbauer, M.: Extracting relevant points of interest from open street map to support E-mobility infrastructure models. Bavarian J. Appl. Sci 4, 323341 (2018). https://doi.org/10.25929/BJAS.V4I1.51
28. Westin, R.B., Manski, C.F.: Theoretical and Conceptual Developments in Demand Modelling. Routledge (1979)
29. Wirges, J., Linder, S., Kessler, A.: Modelling the development of a regional charging infrastructure for electric vehicles in time and space. Eur. J. Transp. Infrastruct. Res. 12(4) (2012). https://doi.org/10.18757/ejtir.2012.12.4.2976, https://journals.open.tudelft.nl/ ejtir/article/view/2976
30. Zhou, Y., et al.: Plug-in electric vehicle market penetration and incentives: a global review. Mitig. Adapt. Strat. Glob. Change 20(5), 777–795 (2014). https://doi.org/10.1007/s11027-014-9611-2

Emergency Management and Response Through 3D Maps and Novel Geo-Information Sources

Iñaki Cejudo(iD), Eider Irigoyen(iD), Harbil Arregui[✉](iD), and Estíbaliz Loyo(iD)

Intelligent Systems for Mobility and Logistics, Vicomtech Foundation, Basque Research and Technology Alliance (BRTA), Mikeletegi 57, Donostia, Spain
{icejudo,eirigoyen,harregui,eloyo}@vicomtech.org
http://www.vicomtech.org

Abstract. Geographical Information Systems (GIS) are essential when representing the Common Operational Picture to have a complete understanding of the situation in disasters. A three-dimensional (3D) representation of the terrain, buildings and surroundings of an emergency area increases the situational awareness of first responders in comparison to the classical 2D map representation when facing the emergency response. This paper describes the architectural solution adopted and the set of functionalities developed to enable: a) timely geolocated representation of near real-time multi-sensor data from heterogeneous sources, b) interaction through a 3D GIS environment for virtual emergency area inspection, c) management of users, scenarios and geospatial elements, and d) advanced geospatial processes. Then, the components that enable the main geospatial capabilities are technically detailed. Finally, validation and evaluation activities carried out with professional first responders and trainees are described together with the results and feedback obtained.

Keywords: Emergency management · Disaster response · Command and control · Location based services

1 Introduction

Maps are a useful means to support Emergency Management and Response (EMR). The shift from 2D to 3D maps represents a notable advancement, aiding first responders in comprehending the emergency environment, with an enhanced view. Including details like terrain slopes and building structures, offers a more comprehensive understanding of the situation. Moreover, novel sensing capabilities and data sources hold immense value in enhancing safety and response efficiency. Notably, cutting-edge tools with real-time indoor and outdoor geolocation and geosensing capabilities are reaching the market. Leveraging these tools, however, poses challenges in dealing with substantial volumes of diverse positioning records, demanding efficient processing, storage, representation, and exploitation techniques. Overcoming these challenges will help maximise the potential benefits of these technological advancements.

First Responders handling disaster response may benefit of advanced Command and Control (CC) solutions that rely on 3D Geographical Information System capabilities. Therefore, the present paper aims to describe the architecture and technology

© The Author(s), under exclusive license to Springer Nature Switzerland AG 2024
C. Grueau et al. (Eds.): GISTAM 2023, CCIS 2107, pp. 92–114, 2024.
https://doi.org/10.1007/978-3-031-60277-1_6

stack chosen to create a 2D/3D geospatial data management solution providing a set of key functionalities in a Command and Control centre during emergency response, extending a previous conference paper [15]. Two main novel additional contributions are presented in this paper. Firstly, the description of technical aspects of the geospatial data management architecture to accommodate new functionalities such as consulting elevation profiles for given routes, visualisation of point clouds and orthophotos have been included. Secondly, the methodology and results of two hands-on activities with first responders are depicted in order to validate the tool in relevant scenarios.

The paper is structured as follows: Sect. 2 describes previous works addressing the problem in the literature and Sect. 3 describes the proposed architecture and functionalities. Then, Sect. 4 and 5 present performance measurements and the validation with end users respectively, followed by the discussion and description of future work in Sect. 6. Finally, Sect. 7 presents the conclusions.

2   Related Work

Diverse first responders collaborate in EMR, each with unique roles and backgrounds. The information must be presented in a comprehensible manner to enhance the decision-making process. Geographical Information Systems (GIS) technology has been shown to be of great help in multiple ways and in various situations such as earthquakes, wildfires, dust storms, health hazards, and terrorism [11]. Based on GIS technology and maps, spatial analysis capabilities support managing the risk and solving the mapping and assessment of hazards, for example, identifying high-hazard regions within given vicinity. It is also interesting in that it provides visual models that help decision-makers make the best use of these advancements.

The interest and preference of end users towards three-dimensional (3D) maps is high, and the study of natural dangers and disasters in 3D has grown significantly during the past few years. 3D maps have the potential to improve the disaster management process according to some authors, since they resolve many perception problems and provide more clearly presented information [13]. User interviews in that study confirmed that young people prefer 3D information. Another study with 71 users concluded that 3D visualisation was considered important by 62% of the users; a rather high result considering that half were not familiar with GIS technology [33].

Enabling 3D navigation for rescuers in unknown indoor and outdoor environments, thanks to accurate 3D positioning, simplifies the logistics of emergency operations [24,34]. Some works have focused on the use of images from Unmanned Aerial Vehicles (UAVs) for 3D modelling. 3D reconstruction of the scene has been proven as a crucial aspect for efficient management of search and rescue efforts [27,31]. Exploiting different heterogeneous sources such as geolocated security cameras and their field of view has also been a topic for other research works [20]. Therefore, supporting 3D maps in the Command and Control Centre, with real-time location information visualisation and analysis is very relevant. Some authors stress, however, that most traditional disaster management systems do not incorporate support for multiple emerging data sources, while the need for real-time big data processing tools that can provide swift and precise outcomes remains unaddressed [29].

In this sense, the availability of geo-information including 3D models of built infrastructures and buildings is becoming common. In addition, diverse up-to-date data with geospatial nature is generated by the most advanced technologies. With the advent of location-based sensors and smartphones equipped with GNSS, the real-time location of First Responders deployed in the field can be monitored. Moreover, satellite and airborne sensors as well as fully fledged Earth Observation solutions such as the Copernicus Emergency Management Service [23] offer large-scale geo-referenced optical, multispectral or Synthetic Aperture Radar [17] imagery for from-above views of disaster areas, while geolocated cameras, sensors and even Light Detection and Ranging (LiDAR) scanners mounted on robots and utility vehicles help inspect and assess the emergency situation from the ground. Combining these potential sources requires robust tools that support geospatial data analysis over time through interactive visualisation.

The exchange and integration of 3D models, point clouds and datasets with 2D spatial data resources, however, is not straightforward. Thus, the definition and usage of standards are important. Some model formats are proprietary, while others have been developed by international standardisation organisations and come from the CAD/BIM, GIS, or Web domains. Both well stabilised and very recent standards for different purposes are found. For instance, the Web Map Service (WMS) is a specification developed by the Open Geospatial Consortium (OGC), that has also become an ISO standard [22], for serving georeferenced map images over the Internet. These images are typically produced by a map server from data provided by a GIS database. At the same time, 3D Tiles is another OGC open standard for massive heterogeneous 3D geospatial datasets such as point clouds, buildings, photogrammetry, and vector data [9]. Substantial efforts to improve interoperability between domains are found in the literature and newly proposed standards such as CityGML 3.0 have the potential to impact integration, between BIM and GIS for instance [30].

Some well-known software solutions implement these and other standards. For instance, Geoserver [21], an open source map server for sharing geospatial data used in some emergency management applications (such as [25]), implements WMS, Web Feature Service (WFS) Web Coverage Service (WCS), and additional protocols like Web Processing Service (WPS) through available extensions. CesiumJS is an open platform that implements 3D Tiles and uses the map engine of WebGL to provide multi-dimensional earth and real terrain display [10]. Some recent works have used this platform for representing virtual situations for urban road emergency training [18]. However, to the authors' knowledge, no other works have presented a platform architecture to be used during emergency response, ready for being integrated with additional data sources in real-time.

3   Solution Description

3.1   Architecture and Components

The solution is formed of a Command and Control (CC) web application, a set of databases, a map serving tool, a set of multiple purpose GIS servers (pointcloud, terrain and elevation) and an API server that hosts the business logic offering the functionalities on top of the emergency database to the web application (Fig. 1). In addition, a set of auxiliary tools and components support other tasks such as user authentication and interaction with external data sources. The proposed solution also includes two client applications relying on augmented reality to offer the first responders deployed in the field an enhanced understanding of their surroundings (for smartphones and smart see-through glasses).

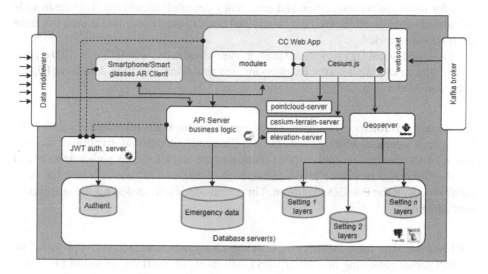

Fig. 1. Architecture diagram of the technology stack.

CC Web App Interface: The proposed solution is a web-based Command and Control application with geospatial visualisation and geocomputation capabilities. Its main objectives are the representation of the area of the scenario and real-time visualisation of the spatial types of data of elements (First Responders, sensors and geolocated resources and risks) that are taking part. Data are obtained from third-party tools that are able to sense, monitor and observe the disaster area from multiple perspectives through different technologies and are made accessible for applications such as the CC Web App interface.

The application includes user management capabilities and emergency inventory management. Two main frameworks have been used to build the application, which are:

- JHipster [28]: Open source development platform to generate, develop and deploy web applications and microservices.
- CesiumJS [10]: Open source javascript library for creating 3D globes and maps. Its main strength is the 3D geospatial visualisation.

Geoserver and Multi-Purpose GIS Servers. Geoserver [21] is a well-known open-source server for sharing geospatial data. It also has geocomputation capabilities. Geoserver implements OGC protocols such as Web Feature Service (WFS), Web Map Service (WMS) or Web Processing Service (WPS) and has been selected as the main map-serving tool for the web-based application. The base map layer contents that are served by Geoserver have been obtained from OpenStreetMap [14]. Geoserver is also used for heatmaps representation and emergency centroid calculation. This centroid is calculated based on all the elements associated with an emergency and is used to centre the map when loaded.

Three additional GIS servers are used: a point cloud server for 3D Tiles, a 3D terrain server, and an elevation server for querying and retrieving elevation data from Digital Elevation Model files.

Relational Databases. The architecture involves one main relational database, the Emergency database, which persists the real-time and historical information of the evolution of the disaster response. Other databases are used for user authentication and for the storage of map base layers information. Postgres [26] was selected for these databases, with the PostGIS extension. This extension is not needed for the authentication database.

API Server. The main business logic of the emergency management is provided by an API server consisting of a set of REST API methods, working on top of the Emergency database, developed in Java Spring Boot [32]. The API server interacts with the elevation server module to obtain the elevation above the sea level of a given pair of geo-coordinates.

Smartphone/Smart Glasses Augmented Reality Client Applications. The CC WebApp interface is complemented with two client application versions for the first responders deployed in the field. They use augmented reality to represent information of the relative location and distance to other first responders, their risk situation and the relative location and distance of georeferenced elements of interest [12].

3.2 Interfaces and Input Data from Other Tools

Data from different sources are received from a middleware system, also developed in the research project but out of the scope of this paper. This system is in charge of the management and fusion of multiple data sources such as sensor information from wearables or drones. It is a bundle of software services with functionalities for data source management and secure data flow among others. The API service developed includes a specific endpoint for each data source and acts as a consumer of this middleware so that the received information can be exploited and persisted in a structured manner.

Apart from this middleware system, a Kafka broker for asynchronous messaging interacts with a websocket used by the CC WebApp to represent received alerts in real-time in the web user interface.

3.3 Main Functionalities Provided

After describing the main components in the previous section, the main functionalities that the CC solution provides are described in the following.

User Management. The concept of user management describes the ability of administrators to manage and configure user access to different IT resources such as services, applications or systems. It is a key concept that enables security and controls who is able to access what information or service. A CC application requires a secure access to handle and interact with all the information and functionalities. This access is granted by the use of user-based authentication.

Scenario Management. The same Command and Control application hosted in a server or an on-premise deployment can be used, in general, to operate in different emergencies and geographical areas. This can occur in different time frames or simultaneously. Therefore, having ways to separate the scenarios is a useful capability. The management of the emergency scenario involves multiple stages in order to setup all the configuration and device resources that need to be associated to the corresponding first responders.

- Creation of a new setting. The concept of "setting" stands for an area where many emergencies can be added. A setting can be, for instance, a country, a state or a city.
- Creation of a new first responder
- Creation of a new emergency. Location, start date and first responders can be specified among other fields.
- Edition of an emergency
- Save a new device
- User configuration where an application user can be assigned to a first responder.
- Adding or removing associations between first responders and devices they may carry or wear.

The creation of a new setting is enabled if separate geographical areas are expected to be covered by a unique deployment of the CC application. This enables the association of each geographical area with the available maps.

Inside a setting, multiple emergencies can be covered simultaneously. Each emergency is focused on a more specific geographical area specified by the limits of a bounding box. Running emergencies are marked as "active" but finished ones and the associated information recorded are persisted for future post-emergency studies. The Emergency Dashboard, Fig. 2, visualises a screenshot of the geographical area map and basic information of each created emergency, and they can be filtered by Scenarios. When any of these emergencies is selected, the application enters in 3D map visualisation view.

Resource and Device Configuration. Multiple and heterogeneous types of resources are usually used in an emergency operation. For instance, first responders are personal resources. In each emergency, a list of first responders is assigned. Other types

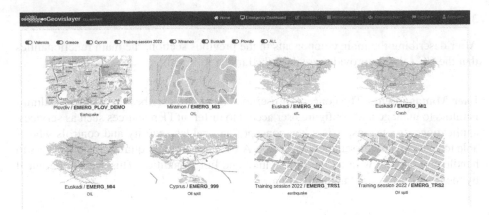

Fig. 2. Emergency Dashboard to select an emergency [15].

of resources can be vehicles, tools, machinery, sensors or other equipment. Sometimes these resources need to be associated to a given first responder. For instance, the information coming from a wearable sensor must be linked to a specific first responder.

Many of the tools developed in the current research project are resources that provide different kinds of data, shared through a common data middleware. This information is represented in the CC application if the correct IDs are associated to the first responder, for instance, if the sensor is providing the health status or positioning of the first responder. However, not all devices need always to be attached to a first responder. We address the following resources or devices providing data: a) Video sources: streaming video from sources like thermal cameras will need to be configured in order to have access to their incoming contents; b) Drones; c) Wearables.

This association between a first responder and a device needs to be done by emergency, since from one emergency to another the personal resources and the devices they will be using could rotate.

Layered 2D, 3D Maps and Road Network Information. Geospatial base layers are key to represent the geographical context where the emergency operation occurs. In summary, a map layer is a GIS component containing groups of points, lines or polygon features that represent real-world entities, or images (like satellite imagery). They help locating what is happening, and where the personnel and technical resources are in relation to other points of interest.

These kinds of layers are provided through Geoserver, the selected open source standalone GIS server which provides the main OGC capabilities to work with 2D spatial tiles in an interoperable way, on top of a PostGIS relational database server. To construct the base 2D maps, contents have been downloaded from OpenStreetMap, and prepared to be served through Geoserver in the form of tiles. The road network information is also extracted from OpenStreetMap and incorporated to the PostGIS database so that Geoserver can also serve it.

With current availability of satellite imagery, a realistic view of the scenario can be offered to the first responders with orthophotos (Fig. 3). Having the capability of showing aerial photographs or satellite imagery can be of much help for situational awareness better understanding the type of terrain, the existence of vegetation, roads or buildings. Orthophotos can be incorporated to the CC solution by using third party online WMS services or by downloading the data and self-hosting it through Geoserver.

Fig. 3. Representation of orthophoto layer [7].

The 3D terrain capabilities are a significant part of the proposed solution. To enable this 3D terrain, a DEM (Digital Elevation Model) of the area to be represented is required. This file is processed in order to create tiles and these are served using the OGC standard Web Map Service (WMS).

Apart from the 3D terrain, the visualisation of point clouds has been included in the solution to enhance emergency perception. Point clouds captured from LiDAR sensors, Fig. 4, give a unique 3D perception of the environment. Figure 5 depicts a combined view of the 3D terrain with orthophoto layers and a representation LiDAR point clouds obtained from a mobile mapping vehicle. In a disaster, machinery equipped with these sensors may be able to inspect the area of interest together with other more traditional sensors such as cameras. Visualizing the reconstruction provided by the point cloud from the CC centre in real-time can help first responders know the situation of the scenario beforehand and evaluate risks and damages prior to sending personal effectives.

Offline Mode. 2D and 3D layers can usually be obtained through third party map service providers, and this is a very usual approach in software applications using maps. But this requires a constant connection to their remote servers. It is quite usual that during an emergency, the access to internet is limited or completely lost. And only a private local network is available to ensure communication among first responders and the emergency management tools. Using self-hosted services such as Geoserver instead of relying on external map providers, the lack of internet connection during the critical situation does not restrict the map usage.

First Responder Localisation and Tracking. This capability enables displaying the position of a first responder over a digital map and see their positions change over time. It is key to ensure the Command and Control operators know where first responders in the field are, with an acceptable delay and an acceptable precision in space. The accuracy of the positioning will strongly depend on the device providing that data, but the Command and Control application will need ensure that it is represented using the

Fig. 4. Representation of point cloud data [1] on top of OpenStreetMap data [6].

Fig. 5. Representation examples of 3D terrain elevation with orthophoto imagery [7] as base layer and LiDAR pointcloud from mobile mapping [1].

correct spatial referencing system. The information of all the geolocated first responders is shown on 2D or 3D maps according to their real-time location, following stabilised refresh-rates, which can be fixed or personalised by each user.

Capabilities for outdoor and indoor localisation are provided by the CC application, for instance, enabling 3D representations of buildings and the location of the first responders at different levels. CesiumJS includes the possibility of representing polygons. For indoor locations of first responders or casualties, buildings can be represented as simple extruded polygons or as specific 3D models created on purpose.

Route Calculation. Route calculation is a functionality that helps obtain an optimal path to reach a final objective position from a given initial position. This optimal path is usually computed as the path that implies the lowest cost. The most common ways of quantifying this cost are distance and travel time. Multiple well-known algorithms exist to obtain optimal or near-optimal results (sometimes a compromise must be found because the computation time to get the best result might be excessive). In general, the input for these algorithms is a set of ways and nodes, modelled as a graph. Having the road network imported as a graph is of high importance in order to be able to compute the shortest paths by using algorithms like Dijkstra [16] and A* [19]. The CC application enables the calculation of the shortest path between two locations. Currently, the changes of the road network due to an incident are not supported but this is a functionality envisioned for the future roadmap of the tool. After requesting a route between two first responders, the computed path is printed on the map, and distance and duration information are displayed.

Elevation Profile. Emergencies sometimes happen in hard-to-reach areas like mountains, forests or neighbourhoods with high slopes. Vehicles or machinery may have problems accessing these areas. Therefore, predefining the intended path and assessing the terrain elevation profile provides valuable information that helps decision-making. This functionality permits a user to draw a path as a sequence of consecutive points on the web application map (following the route path provided by the previous functionality or not) and request the system to compute and display the elevation profile, as shown in Fig. 6. Besides that, when clicking the graphic, the following additional metrics are calculated and shown in the web application: maximum uphill and downhill gradients, percentage of route with uphill gradient, average uphill gradient, percentage of route considered flat (elevation between -3% and 3%), average flat gradient, percentage of route with downhill gradient, average downhill gradient, and a 2D plot of the elevation profile.

Cataloging and Location of Necessary Equipment and Geospatial Elements. The CC application supports the creation of geospatial elements of interest by drawing them on a map. These can be generic "POINT", "LINE" or "POLYGON" shape types of elements. This allows displaying them on the map in client applications carried by first responders in the field. For instance, the Inventory creation functionality provided by the CC application acts as an authoring tool that creates geospatial entities that are then

Fig. 6. Calculated elevation profile of a route.

displayed within the assigned emergency, and can be used by any other application that uses the API, such as the augmented reality smartphone and see-through glasses clients. In addition to the shape type, currently, the elements can be categorised into Resources, Citizens in Risk, Danger Area, Alerts or Mobile Command and Control Centre location. The user is able to draw the element on the map and it is then saved in the system with associated details.

Real-Time Environmental and First Responders' Health Status Through Sensor Data Visualisation. Via third party tools, the data collected by multiple wearable sensors and centralised by the data logger are shared through the middleware system. This information gives valuable insights of the situation of the first responders' safety, apart from the localisation data that has previously been addressed. In addition, it enables quickly alerting the commanders to a potentially injured FR and it provides actionable intelligence without needing audio or visual communication between the FR and their commander.

Drone Flight Plan and Telemetry Visualisation. Drones are another key part of emergency management nowadays. These are very valuable resources that help operations from an aerial perspective. Integrating their information in Command and Control applications is very useful. In the proposed solution, via the middleware system, telemetry information of the drones are shared with the Command and Control application in order to display their status and position in real time. For instance, the CC application is capable of displaying and updating the position with a given refresh rate. The main purpose of this functionality is not handling the flight mission, which needs a very frequent and critical monitoring to guarantee the safety of the UAV and the personnel involved but following their approximate situation in context with the rest of the elements and resources being part of the emergency operation. In Fig. 7, the position and details of a flying drone are represented on the map. Since the CC application allows 3D visualisation of the scene, apart from the 2D positions, the elevation can be represented. Moreover, showing or hiding the expected flight plan is enabled.

Fig. 7. Flying drone details with activated visualisation of the flight plan [15].

Alerts. The management of alerts is key to allow acting fast and efficiently in decision-making. This is valid for first responders in the Command and Control Centre and for the ones deployed in the field. Displaying alerts that require attention from a responsible at the Command and Control Centre is an important functionality. In general, alerts are expected to be shared through the middleware system. In addition, a specific component enables subscription to Common Alerting Protocol servers provided by authorised entities.

Post-Emergency Functionalities. The post-emergency management of the collected information helps to understand and evaluate the emergency response, once finished. The following functionalities are given:

- Statistics dashboards: Interactive charts and tables about statistics of alarms, numbers of exchanged messages, number of injured people treated.
- Reporting: Creation of summary reports about the evolution of the emergency from the beginning to the end.
- Geospatial statistics: This helps understanding the movements of first responders in the field, extracting quantitative data about areas visited, distances they have traveled, time to reach some locations, time they have spent in a dangerous zone, and so on. Visual representations such as charts and heatmaps are used (Fig. 8).

3.4 Technical Description

Even though the web application provides generalistic user administration and accounts-related functionalities, the main technical particularities belong to functions involving the visual components that show the emergency dashboard, the components that enable the user interaction to create new shapes associated with an emergency and all the components that allow 3D geospatial visualisation and interaction capabilities. In the following, we describe their technical considerations.

Fig. 8. Heatmap with positions from a selected first responder [15].

Cesium as the Core GIS Component. The main web interface component is where the emergency map and information are embedded in the website, using CesiumJS, an open source javascript library for creating 3D globes and maps.

When an emergency is selected in the emergency dashboard, this component automatically loads. Cesium's *WebMapServiceImageryProvider* function loads a base map for the world globe and a detailed map of the emergency setting from Geoserver. In the process of loading the component, there are three types of API requests that are invoked to retrieve emergency-associated data: 1) calls made only once, when the component loads, 2) calls made when the component loads and whenever the information is updated and 3) calls made when the operator selects a specific entity on the map.

Once the main component has loaded and the initial information has been retrieved from the API, the first operation that is done is an initial camera flight to the centre of the bounding rectangle of the emergency. For this operation, Cesium's *CameraFlyTo* function is used and the coordinates are obtained from an API call that computes the minimum bounding box that covers the last positions of all the geolocated elements in the selected emergency.

The World globe, map layers and emergency entities are visualised using Cesium's Viewer component. Any Cesium function has to be inside this component. Cesium has different kind of components for visualizing Entities. The ones used in this application are the following:

- *ModelGraphics*: loads 3D models in glTF format (drones, buildings, ...).
- *PolylineGraphics*: used for representing drone flight plan, line shape of interest, and route information.
- *BillboardGraphics*: loads an image representing a first responder type or any other point as a shape of interest.
- *LabelGraphics*: used for showing a first responder's code.
- *PolygonGraphics*: used for showing polygon shape of interest.
- *PointGraphics*: used for representing drone's mission waypoints.
- *WallGraphics*: used for representing route elevation profile.

Using *WebMapServiceImageryProvider* as well, a heatmap layer of positions of first responders can be represented. This layer is created in Geoserver applying a transformation to a style.

For interaction with the 2D and 3D maps, the user can move the view in any direction and can select any entity displayed in the viewer. When an entity is selected, a description is shown with *EntityDescription* component. There is also a menu function called "Zoom to" where user can redirect the camera to any first responder or shape of interest in the emergency. Cesium's *CameraFlyTo* function is used, as for the initial camera position. There is an specific component for creation of new shapes in the emergency. Cesium viewer's 3D globe is loaded, an the user can select what emergency wants to work on. The user can manually draw point, line or polygon shapes in any place of the map, assign a category to the shape and save it. Cesium has a *ScreenSpaceEventHandler* function for managing user clicks over the Cesium Viewer. Once the new shapes are saved, they are included in the Emergency Database and can be visualised using the CC application or any other application that uses the API.

Geoserver Map Creation Process and Usage. The process for serving a map with Geoserver starts obtaining an OpenStreetMap file of the wanted area. This map has to be processed into a PostGIS database with Imposm tool [4]. Applying a specific mapping in Imposm, converts the map information into several database tables. Then, Geoserver allows to import these tables. Each one works as a layer in Geoserver. For visualizing a layer like a typical map, a specific style has to be applied to each layer. For the creation of the whole map, a custom selection of layers has been chosen. The desired layers must be grouped into a "layer group". The order in which the layers are added when creating this group is important. Once the map is created, it is served to the CC application by WMS (Web Map Service) standard. Orthophoto layers are also served offline if needed. Even though they can be requested through existing third party WMS services, having them stored and served locally reduces dependency on internet connection. Imagery is, therefore, downloaded and self-hosted in Geoserver and visualised in Cesium as another map layer. In Geoserver, a new "store" of type Raster Data Source must be created with the orthophotos data previously stored in GeoTIFF format. Cesium's *WebMapServiceImageryProvider* function loads the map as another 2D map.

Cesium-Terrain-Server Preparation and Usage. Apart from imagery layers for 2D maps, the solution includes 3D terrain layers that are supported by a specific separate GIS server. In our case, we import 3D terrain using *CesiumTerrainProvider* function. Cesium accepts heightmap or quantized-mesh type tiles. The latter is more optimised for rendering. To process and create the tiles the *cesium-terrain-builder-docker* [2] utility is used. Afterwards, in order to serve the tiles, the *cesium-terrain-server* [3] utility is used. The *CesiumTerrainProvider* component will then be able to load the terrain from the URL provided by the *cesium-terrain-server* server.

Pointcloud-Server Preparation and Usage. The process of visualising the point cloud starts with obtaining or downloading point cloud data. A standard format for this data is LAZ format, a compressed LiDAR Data Exchange file. The next step is to merge the input LAZ file or set of multiple files into a single LAS file, a format designed to interchange LiDAR point cloud data. Some open-source projects have been used to build the pipeline used by the solution. *LAStools* [5] is an open-source tool for LiDAR processing that permits this operation among others. Then, to convert a LAS file into 3D tiles, *Py3dtiles* [8] is used. Finally, a static 3D tiles server serves these tiles to view the point cloud using Cesium's *Cesium3DTileset* function. The process has many steps, therefore an automated pipeline has been prepared, where the only interaction the application user has to make is to select the point cloud data folder that stores the data files to be served in LAZ format. Then, the process operations are automatically executed, as depicted in Fig. 9, and when the web interface is refreshed, the point cloud can be visualised. The options menu has functions to adjust the point cloud height to correct any deviations with the existing terrain and make a camera flight to it.

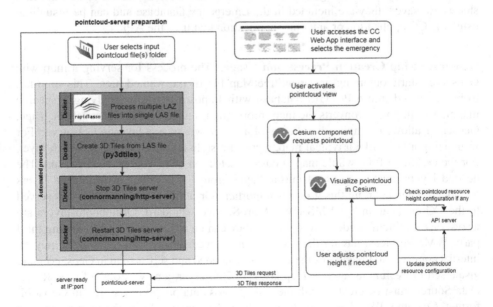

Fig. 9. Pipeline for the configuration and usage of point cloud data.

Elevation-Server Preparation and Usage. The elevation-server is used by the main API when a elevation profile is requested. This server has to be fed with elevation data in HGT format. HGT files are Shuttle Radar Topography Mission (SRTM) data files and can be downloaded from several sources. The selected sequence of path points marked on the map of the user interface are sent to the API server to request an elevation profile. For each of the path points, the API requests the nearest reference point value of the altitude above sea level to the elevation-server. The result of the elevation profile query is represented in the CC web application through a Cesium *WallGraphics* component, and the height of the graphic corresponds to the elevation absolute values.

4   Performance Evaluation

The performance of the multiple tasks and functionalities is affected by the number of records. How this size would affect the interaction of the user with the application or the feasibility of ingesting and presenting real-time data sources needs to be evaluated. In the following, we present the processing time required for two types of tasks, under a Ubuntu 18 8 GB RAM, Intel Core i5-9400F CPU @ 2.90 GHz.

4.1   Processing of First Responder Locations

One of the features of the CC application is the initial flight described in Sect. 3.4. To calculate the bounding box of the last positions received from the first responders deployed in an emergency, a custom API method has been implemented based on Post-GIS. Another way to calculate the bounding box is to make use of one of the WPS functions provided by Geoserver. The processing times of both methods are compared.

The main factor that affects the processing time is the number of location records in the database and this is linked to: a) the rate at which data is sent by each first responder equipment, b) the duration of the data collection, and c) the total number of first responders sending location information. Tests have been performed for rates ranging from 20, 30, 60 and 300 s, data collections for 3 and 5 h and 1, 5, 15 and 25 first responders.

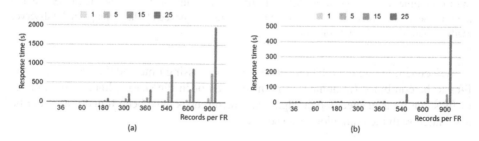

Fig. 10. Response time comparison for different number of first responders (1, 5, 15, 25) and according to the number for records per FR, depending on the method: a) API. b) Geoserver.

Results show that the response time increases exponentially from 300 records per FR in the case of the API and from 540 records per FR in the case of Geoserver (Fig. 10). Focusing on scenarios with more records, the response of the API, in the worst case, is 2746% slower than Geoserver's (the case of 1 record every minute during 5 h with 25 first responders). Therefore, as future work, it is necessary to make the implementation of the API more efficient in order to improve scalability.

4.2   Processing of LiDAR Point Clouds

Processing multiple point cloud files to make them available for their consumption in the CC application requires some time. In order to understand the impact of the size and number of files to have the pointcloud-server ready to use by the Cesium component, we have measured the processing time for a set of point cloud files of different size and types. Figure 11 shows the performance evaluation in processing time for partial steps (a) and the total process (b) before the server is up and running. Two different LiDAR open data sources have been compared to check possible differences due to the capturing method or the format: aerial ("LiDAR 2ª Cobertura" [7]) and terrestrial from mobile mapping ("2019 Mobile Mapping" [1]).

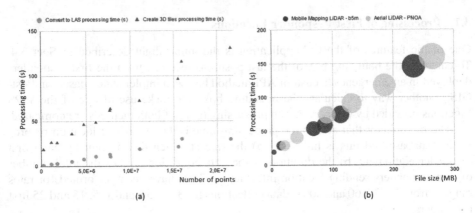

Fig. 11. a) Processing time of point cloud files sets of different size (in number of points) according to the time needed to convert different different files into a single converted LAS file and the time needed to create 3D tiles. b) Total processing time needed to have the pointcloud-server ready, separating by the type of source.

We conclude that the relation between the processing time and the total size of the files to be combined (in number of point records or in file size) is linear. The number of files can be neglected and no significant differences have been found that could be associated with the point cloud data source.

5   Validation with First Responders

The proposed solution has been validated in two events simulating disaster management operational environments: a) the final project pilot held in the port of Valencia (Spain) where the solution was used in combination with other complementary solutions developed by project consortium partners under a larger project platform architecture and b) a session with a training centre for First Responders in Brunete (Spain).

5.1 Port Environment Exercise

The last training and pilot of the RESPOND-A project respectively took place on the 15th and 16th of February 2023 in the port of Valencia (Spain), Fig. 12. This final demonstration was a coordinated effort led by Fundación Valenciaport and the Valencia Local Police involving the project consortium as well as local organisations (Valencia Port Police, Firefighters, Mooring Services, Spanish Red Cross and Civil Protection). A total of approximately 150 participants were involved in the demonstration which simulated a traffic accident causing fire and oil spill - a type of hazard which can have very serious consequences on the personnel involved, critical infrastructures as well as the ecosystem.

The exercise consisted in managing the emergency to respond to a traffic accident between two trucks in the port surroundings causing fire and heavy smoke. As a consequence of the crash, the oil coming from one of the trucks fell into the sea. Therefore, the emergency response also had to contemplate the contention of the split oil floating on the water surface.

(a)   (b)

Fig. 12. a) Aerial view of the pilot site in Valencia Port, Spain (PNOA imagery [7]). b) One moment of the pilot exercise with the first responders deployed in the field.

The 3D GIS CC WebApp described in the present work was part of a joint deployment of a wide set of project components including health and environmental sensors, smart wearable sensors, augmented and virtual reality devices and applications, reconnaissance and firefighting robots, drones, 5G connectivity and other Command and Control applications to enable communications and Common Operational Picture capabilities, increasing the situational awareness of First Responders in the field and those at the advanced command centre. The next key functions were specifically covered by the solution twice, during the first day as a training/rehearsal and during the second day as the pilot execution itself:

- The surroundings and 3D building models of the port area and the city were displayed.
- Weather alerts published by the Common Alerting Protocol were being received (non-existing at the moment of the pilot execution, and thus not reported).
- Bathymetry lines of the coastline were displayed.
- The real-time location and elevation of the drone were represented as it moved to obtain video images of the emergency area.
- The command centre operator draw the polygon of the current extension of the oil spill according to what the video from the drone was showing.
- The smart see-through glasses AR client application collected the real-time location of a first responder deployed in the field and that was displayed on the map at the CC centre.
- The smartphone AR client application collected the real-time location of a first responder deployed in the field, which was displayed on the map at the CC centre, and showed the extension of the oil spill through AR visualisation.

The exercise was satisfactory and all objectives were met and demonstrated.

5.2 Training Centre Exercise

The session with a training centre for First Responders took place on the 9th and 10th of May 2023 in the VIGILES Institute, Brunete (Spain). VIGILES is a Civil Protection Institute for vocational education in civil protection and emergencies. The CC application was tested with over 30 people, including students and professionals. It was a two-day session.

During the first day session, all participants signed the consents, received a theoretical training and watched a demo of the tools (the CC WebApp and the AR Client applications) given by the researchers, and tested the installation of the software.

On the second day, exercises simulating real situations were performed in a properly prepared training camp. Next to the camp, there was a specific area where a big screen for the CC centre was installed, depicted in Fig. 13.

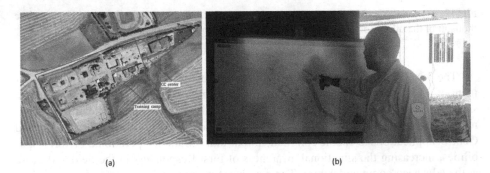

(a)   (b)

Fig. 13. a) Aerial view of the training camp in Brunete, Spain (PNOA imagery [7]). b) CC centre during training exercise.

Tests consisted of three exercises with First Responder trainees divided into groups. The three exercises were repeated twice with different participants. The smartphone AR Client application installed in participants' devices tracked the location of First Responders and helped with searching tasks. One set of smart see-through glasses was used by one participant in each exercise. The exercises were:

- Standard search: Half of the group hid and the other half had to search. The CC centre monitored the situation while metrics were obtained.
- Guided search: Half of the group hid and the other half had to search. From the CC centre, there was direct communication by walkie-talkies to guide the search.
- Blind search with obstacles: Half of the group hid without location tracking and the other half had to search. When a searcher found a hidden "victim", they had to take the "victim" back to the CC centre, avoiding some dangerous areas drawn by the CC application operator. The rescuers were informed of the dangerous areas through the smartphone AR client.

At the end of the second day session, an extensive questionnaire assessing the used tools was filled out by the participants. The questionnaire had 23 questions about user experience, features, applicability and suggestions related to the CC WebApp. Figure 14 shows a set of the most representative questions and the responses collected.

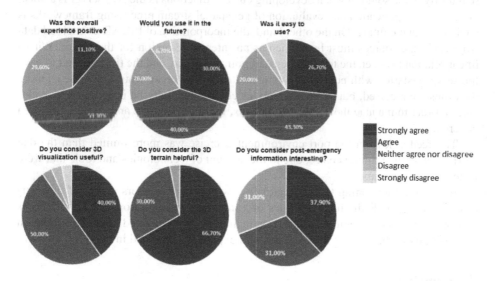

Fig. 14. Summary of evaluation results.

The following findings were extracted from the feedback of 31 questionnaire respondents:

- Regarding the professional future of the participants, 83% were focused on firefighting, 13% on search and rescue, and 4% on other tasks.

- The majority of them (70%) considered the CC web app is an easy-to-use tool and were interested in using it in the future.
- Over 85% of the people answered that 3D visualisation, 3D models and 3D terrain were crucial features for successful emergency response.
- Route calculation had the support of over 80% of the respondents.
- Although the creation of new elements had great acceptance, 11% of the participants answered that it was not easy to use.
- The information visualised in the CC web app was considered enough to give proper indications to First Responders in the field by 63%
- Most of them coincided with having real-time wind data would be a valuable add-on.
- Most of them coincided with being able to send specific alerts from the CC centre to First Responders in the field would be a valuable add-on.

6 Discussion and Future Work

The evaluation of the performance tests demonstrated the quantitative impact of the amount of records and the frequency of sensor data captured when performing geospatial tasks and GIS server preparations such as the pointcloud-server in order to operate the web 3D GIS application. One hand, it has been demonstrated that working on the scalability of the solution when developing custom functions in the API server is a must. To do so, the application and evaluation of geospatial stream processing frameworks is envisioned in the future. On the other hand, the incorporation of LiDAR pointcloud data from real-time sources must be studied as an interesting option for the future. With a linear relation between the total aggregated pointcloud size and the time needed to have the server restarted with new data, this would imply the delay would increase as more data files are received, but some alternatives could potentially be proposed and evaluated in order to manage the history of the files, according to time and space of the area covered.

The feedback from the port environment exercise was more limited than the one carried out in the training centre, due to the amount of technologies and tools that were tested at the same time.

It is worth mentioning that the validation with first responders in any of the exercises did not include the functionalities of point cloud visualisation, elevation profiles and orthophoto visualisation. In fact, this features were developed after the validation exercises, partly because of the feedback and experience obtained in them.

7 Conclusions

This paper has described a CC web application based on 3D maps integrating novel and diverse geo-information sources for first responders in EMR. The description includes the functional applicability in disaster management by first responders operating the solution in a control centre, as well as the architectural and technical aspects that enable the integration and interaction of the end user with the tool.

The proposed components and overall structure of the 3D maps solution, which can be expanded for utilization in various CC contexts outside of emergency management, have been developed to interact with data coming from different heterogeneous sources and have been validated in relevant scenarios with positive feedback from professionals and trainees. These validation activities inspired to incorporate the latest innovations such as the inclusion of elevation profile calculation and point cloud visualisation, which were not developed (and thus were not tested by the end users) during validation activities. The solution acceptance by the trainees, without those features, was already high (90% of the respondents agreed or strongly agreed that the 3D visualisation was helpful; 70% of the respondents agreed or strongly agreed that they would like to use it in the future). This feedback, which comes from young adults used to new technologies that will become professional first responders in the near future, has been found positive and encourages the work on improving the performance of the solution, making the usage more intuitive and incorporating new functionality.

Acknowledgements. The research work presented in this article has been supported by the European Commission under the Horizon 2020 Programme, through funding of the RESPOND-A project (G.A. 883371).

References

1. b5m Infraestructura de Datos Espaciales de Gipuzkoa. https://b5m.gipuzkoa.eus/web5000/es. Accessed 03 Aug 2023
2. Cesium Terrain Builder. https://github.com/tum-gis/cesium-terrain-builder-docker. Accessed 24 Nov 2022
3. Cesium Terrain Server. https://github.com/geo-data/cesium-terrain-server. Accessed 24 Nov 2022
4. ImpOSM. https://imposm.org/. Accessed 24 Nov 2022
5. LAStools. https://github.com/LAStools/LAStools. Accessed 03 Aug 2023
6. OpenStreetMap contributors. http://planet.openstreetmap.org. Planet dump [Data file from 15 Nov 2021]
7. Plan Nacional de Ortofotografía Aérea (PNOA) - Instituto Geográfico Nacional (IGN). https://www.ign.es/web/ign/portal. Accessed 03 Aug 2023
8. Py3dtiles. https://gitlab.com/Oslandia/py3dtiles. Accessed 03 Aug 2023
9. 3D Tiles (2022). https://www.ogc.org/standard/3dtiles/. Accessed 03 July 2023
10. Cesium JS, 3D geospatial visualization for the web (2022). https://cesium.com/platform/cesiumjs/. Accessed 24 Nov 2022
11. Abdalla, R.: Evaluation of spatial analysis application for urban emergency management. SpringerPlus **5** (2016). https://doi.org/10.1186/s40064-016-3723-y
12. Arregui, H., et al.: An augmented reality framework for first responders: the RESPOND-a project approach, pp. 1–6, December 2022. https://doi.org/10.1109/PACET56979.2022.9976376
13. Bandrova, T., Zlatanova, S., Konečný, M.: Three-dimensional maps for disaster management, vol. I-4, July 2012. https://doi.org/10.5194/isprsannals-I-4-245-2012
14. Bennet, J.: OpenStreetMap. Packt Publishing Ltd, Birmingham (2010)
15. Cejudo, I., Irigoyen, E., Arregui, H., Loyo, E.: 3D geospatial data management architecture for common operational picture functionalities in emergency response. In: Grueau, C., Rodrigues, A., Ragia, L. (eds.) Proceedings of the 9th International Conference on Geographical Information Systems Theory, Applications and Management, GISTAM 2023, Prague, Czech Republic, 25–27 April 2023, pp. 48–59. SCITEPRESS (2023). https://doi.org/10.5220/0011837800003473

16. Dijkstra, E.W.: A note on two problems in connexion with graphs. Numer. Math. **1**(1), 269–271 (1959)
17. Ezquerro, P., et al.: Analysis of SAR-derived products to support emergency management during volcanic crisis: La Palma case study. Remote Sens. Environ. **295**, 113668 (2023). https://doi.org/10.1016/j.rse.2023.113668. https://www.sciencedirect.com/science/article/pii/S0034425723002195
18. Gao, X., Zhang, J., Zou, R., Li, J., Cao, Z.: Multi-user collaborative virtual emergency drill system for urban road emergencies. ISPRS Ann. Photogram. Remote Sensing Spat. Inf. Sci. **X-3/W2-2022**, 9–15 (2022). https://doi.org/10.5194/isprs-annals-X-3-W2-2022-9-2022. https://www.isprs-ann-photogramm-remote-sens-spatial-inf-sci.net/X-3-W2-2022/9/2022/
19. Hart, P., Nilsson, N., Raphael, B.: A formal basis for the heuristic determination of minimum cost paths. IEEE Trans. Syst. Sci. Cybernet. **4**(2), 100–107 (1968). https://doi.org/10.1109/tssc.1968.300136
20. Hong, J.H., Lu, Y.H., Chen, C.H.: The use of CCTV in the emergency response: a 3D GIS perspective. Int. Arch. Photogramm. Remote Sens. Spat. Inf. Sci. **42**, 19–25 (2019)
21. Iacovella, S.: GeoServer Beginner's Guide: Share Geospatial Data Using Open Source Standards. Packt Publishing Ltd, Birmingham (2017)
22. Jagusiak, B., Pokorski, G.: Application of transport security system symbology for emergency mass notification systems. Transp. Probl. Int. Sci. J. **17**(3) (2022)
23. Jutz, S., Milagro-Pérez, M.: Copernicus: the European Earth Observation programme. Revista de Teledetección (56), V–XI (2020)
24. Kolawole, O., Hunukumbure, M.: A drone-based 3D localization solution for emergency services. In: ICC 2022-IEEE International Conference on Communications, pp. 1–6. IEEE (2022)
25. Li, B., Wu, J., Pan, M., Huang, J.: Application of 3D WebGIS and real-time technique in earthquake information publishing and visualization. Earthq. Sci. **28**, 223–231 (2015). https://doi.org/10.1007/s11589-015-0124-1
26. Momjian, B.: PostgreSQL: Introduction and Concepts. Addison-Wesley Longman Publishing Co. Inc., Boston (2001)
27. Mysiris, P., Doulamis, N., Doulamis, A., Sourlas, V., Amditis, A.: Pervasive 3D reconstruction to identify hidden 3D survival spaces for search and rescue management. In: 2018 IEEE 16th International Conference on Dependable, Autonomic and Secure Computing, 16th International Conference on Pervasive Intelligence and Computing, 4th International Conference on Big Data Intelligence and Computing and Cyber Science and Technology Congress, pp. 808–813 (2018). https://doi.org/10.1109/DASC/PiCom/DataCom/CyberSciTec.2018.00-25
28. Raible, M.: The JHipster Mini-Book. Lulu.com (2016)
29. Shah, S.A., Seker, D.Z., Hameed, S., Draheim, D.: The rising role of big data analytics and IoT in disaster management: recent advances, taxonomy and prospects. IEEE Access **7**, 54595–54614 (2019). https://doi.org/10.1109/ACCESS.2019.2913340
30. Tan, Y., Liang, Y., Zhu, J.: CityGML in the Integration of BIM and the GIS: challenges and Opportunities. Buildings **13**(7) (2023). https://doi.org/10.3390/buildings13071758. https://www.mdpi.com/2075-5309/13/7/1758
31. Verykokou, S., Ioannidis, C., Athanasiou, G., Doulamis, N., Amditis, A.: 3D reconstruction of disaster scenes for urban search and rescue. Multimedia Tools Appl. **77** (2018). https://doi.org/10.1007/s11042-017-5450-y
32. Walls, C.: Spring Boot in Action, 1st edn. Manning Publications Co., New York City (2016)
33. Zlatanova, S.: SII for emergency response: the 3D challenges, June 2008
34. Zlatanova, S., Oosterom, P., Verbree, E.: 3D technology for improving disaster management: geo-DBMS and positioning. In: Proceedings of the IEEE - PIEEE, July 2004

Author Index

C. Grueau et al. (Eds.): GISTAM 2023, CCIS 2107, p. 115, 2024.
https://doi.org/10.1007/978-3-031-60277-1

© The Editor(s) (if applicable) and The Author(s), under exclusive license to Springer Nature Switzerland AG 2024
C. Grübner et al. (eds.), *Title*, https://doi.org/10.1007/978-3-031-60276-4
https://doi.org/10.1007/978-3-031-60276-4

Printed in the United States
by Baker & Taylor Publisher Services